# Inspirations for the Man of Valour

# Inspirations for the Man of Valour

by

Oluwakemi Ola-Ojo © 2015

INSPIRATIONS FOR THE MAN OF VALOUR

**Inspirations for the Man of Valour.**
ISBN 978-1-908-015-12-9

Copyright© 2015 by Oluwakemi O. Ola-Ojo

*All publishing rights belong exclusively to Protokos Publishers.*

Published by
**Protokos Publishers**
Website:www.protokospublishers.com
email: protokospublishers@aol.co.uk

Printed in United Kingdom.

*All rights reserved under International Copyright Law.*
*Contents and/or cover may not be reproduced, stored in a retrieval system, or be transmitted, in whole or in part in any form, or by any means, electronic, mechanical or photocopying or otherwise without the express written consent of the Publisher.*

## ACKNOWLEDGEMENT

Many wonderful, loving and caring people have been a blessing to me especially in this ministry of reaching out and sharing God's love.

I am especially grateful to God who made our paths to meet and I am thankful to each person whose support and love has made it possible for me to write.

Thank you to everyone who corrected and made suggestions to the publishing of this book.

To my editor, Mrs. `Sumbo Oladipo who worked tirelessly on this book and many others. I pray for God's anointing to increase more and more upon your life in Jesus' name.

Finally but not in the least, to the wonderful team at Protokos Publishers for working round the clock to get this book published and market my books.

I appreciate you all.

## DEDICATION

To my best Friend and Mentor,
One who gives me the inspiration,
He gives me the courage and strength to write.
– 'Sweet Holy Spirit'

Please help me to appreciate Him even now!

## CONTENTS

| | | |
|---|---|---|
| Acknowledgement | | V |
| Dedication | | VI |
| Introduction | | X |
| 1. | **Praise Him for His Love and Favour** | XIV |
| | • What shall I render? | 15 |
| | • At the cross | 17 |
| | • God's love like the sun | 19 |
| 2. | **Led by the Spirit of God** | 20 |
| | • It's a matter of your look | 21 |
| | • Looking at the outside | 23 |
| | • Your approval is required | 25 |
| 3. | **Watchfulness** | 27 |
| | • Keep awake | 28 |
| | • Family plan | 29 |
| | • Costly mistake | 32 |
| | • Train them or lose them | 34 |
| | • I loved them both dearly | 35 |
| 4 | **Consecration and Intimacy with God** | 38 |
| | • Thy will be done O Lord | 39 |
| | • Alone with God | 42 |
| | • I'd love to see my Saviour | 44 |

|   |                                          |     |
|---|------------------------------------------|-----|
|   | • Isaac must go                          | 45  |
|   | • Take time                              | 47  |
|   | • Open Lord                              | 51  |
| 5 | **Faith in God**                         | **52** |
|   | • As a man thinks                        | 53  |
|   | • At life's edge                         | 55  |
|   | • But whose report do you believe?       | 57  |
|   | • Casting all upon him                   | 59  |
|   | • I will lift up my eyes                 | 61  |
|   | • Looking up to heaven                   | 64  |
| 6 | **His Call**                             | **66** |
|   | • What is your calling?                  | 67  |
|   | • He makes us go                         | 69  |
|   | • Can He use you?                        | 71  |
|   | • Identification seal                    | 73  |
|   | • The man called Joseph                  | 75  |
| 7 | **The All-Sufficient and Benevolent God**| **77** |
|   | • The cafeteria                          | 78  |
|   | • God's provision                        | 81  |
|   | • Jesus has the power                    | 83  |
|   | • My unlimited God                       | 84  |
|   | • God's greatness                        | 88  |
|   | • Prepare to receive from God            | 90  |
| 8 | **God's Salvation Plan**                 | **92** |

- Death — 93
- He forgave me — 95
- Behold the world shaker! — 97
- The beauty of the snow — 99

## 9  Facing the Challenges of Life — 101
- Facing the problem — 102
- Not an easy road — 104
- Blessed be the name of the Lord — 105
- The tides — 106

## 10  Wisdom for living — 108
- No careless word — 109
- The appointed time of the Lord — 111
- Touch someone today — 113

## 11. The Awesome and Omnipotent God — 115
- Name — 116
- God to the professionals — 118
- Just a touch — 120
- The same good Lord made them all — 121
- Do you know yourself — 122
- Opportunity to Become a Christian — 125
- Other Books — 127
- Useful Links — 147

# INTRODUCTION

This book of poetic and inspiration has been written to complement the other books in the three part series titled 'Good Dads, Bad Dads'. As its name suggests, it is a collection of poems and inspirations that I feel are applicable to all, especially men, fathers, brothers, uncles, nephews and friends to read, meditate upon and share with others if possible. The poems cover a range of topics and issues many of which are peculiar to men.

The title for this book is taken from Judges 6 verse 12. Godliness exalts a nation but sin is a reproach to any people. Sin will always lead to oppression and slavery. God's choice of a deliverer for that season in the history of the Israelites was timid and fearful Gideon who con sidered himself as insignificant and from the smallest tribe. Unknown to him and, within him was all that was necessary to conquer the enemy and set himself, family and people free.

God often does not use the qualified but qualifies those He calls. He calls the foolish to shame the wise and the weak to shame the strong ones. Gideon knew the national history, heard about God's deliverance in this past, could not comprehend how and when God will rescue his people and through whom.

By reason of fear, he was threshing wheat in the wine press but he was very observant and hospitable. An angel of the Lord appeared to him. He checked to confirm that it was God who was speaking to him indeed and, he obeyed God even in the face of a possible death penalty for destroying the idols of Baal.

You may have been praying for a change either in your finances, home, job, community, etc. God is able to use you, even you, your circumstances notwithstanding, to deliver yourself, family and community from every yoke of oppression, bondage and slavery in Jesus' name. There may be some family or community idols to destroy, a Godly altar to build, oppositions to withstand from your close ones and relations but arise from your hiding and timidity to destroy all the works of the enemy in your life, family and community.

Brother, father, uncle and nephew, God's hand and anointing is upon you as you seek His face to hear and to obey Him only. Arise, great man of courage in the name of Jesus Christ, in the strength and anointing of the Lord. It is your time to be free and bring freedom to others.

These poems are for my reading audience especially all the men. They have been written over the years to encourage, motivate and challenge us all. The poems could be used as 'ice breakers or crackers' in a discussion group, amongst friends and colleagues. They may also be used as tools for leading others to Jesus Christ or for counselling in the Christian journey. I pray that you find them refreshing and encouraging in Jesus' name. Amen.

Bible references have been provided at the end of most of the poems for those who would want to study the subject being discussed more.

On behalf on every mother, sister, wife, daughter, aunt and niece, I celebrate and appreciate you my brother(s). May the Lord bless you, lift His countenance upon you, grant you His peace and a resounding success in all of your undertakings from now in Jesus' name.

As these poems are applicable to either male or female, I will be using the male gender for ease of writing and reading.

# 1

# *Praise Him for His love and favour*

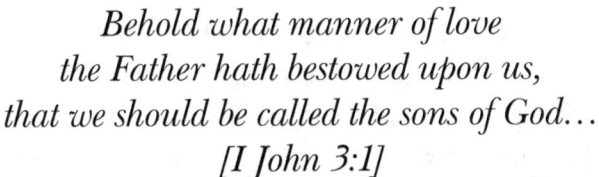

*Behold what manner of love
the Father hath bestowed upon us,
that we should be called the sons of God…
[I John 3:1]*

*Bless the Lord, O my soul, and forget not all
His benefits…
[Psalms 103:2 (KJV)]*

# WHAT SHALL I RENDER?

What shall I render to You my Lord?
For making me wonderfully complex,
With ears to hear, nose to breathe,
Mouth to eat, eyes to see,
Legs to walk, hands to hold and write.

What shall I render to You my Lord?
For creating me in Your own very image,
For making me your child through Jesus Christ,
For cleansing me from my sins and guilt through His blood,
For giving me life in abundance through His love.

What shall I render to You my Lord?
For giving me fresh air to breathe,
For giving me water to drink, cook and wash,
For giving me all kinds of fruits and food to eat,
For giving me good health to enjoy them all.

What shall I render to You my Lord?
For my loving and caring parents,
For my understanding brothers and sisters,
For my very nice neighbours and friends,
For my tolerant colleagues at work.

What shall I render to You my Lord?
For my faithful and loving husband,
For my hardworking and understanding spouse,
For my God-fearing and obedient children,
For my caring and pleasant in-laws.

What shall I render to You my Lord?
For the clothes, which keep me warm?
For the shelter in which I reside and I'm protected,
For the sun and moon which gives me light,
For the rain, which gives me water?

What shall I render to You my Lord?
For all these blessings told and untold,
I will forever give You my thanks,
Telling others about Your wonderful love,
And praising You with all I have. [1]

---

[1] Psalm 116:12-14

# AT THE CROSS

At the cross God's unlimited love was shown,
Jesus Christ's humility and obedience to God's was proved,
His example of sincere and divine love to mankind was demonstrated,
It was a place of final and complete exchange of life,
His sinless life was exchanged for mankind's sinful lives.

At the cross was a place for new and permanent contract,
Written and sealed with the sinless blood of the lamb,
With Christ declaring and shouting it is finished beloved.
Finished with sin, sickness, death, satan and his emissaries,
With open access to God the father, unlike before his death.

At the cross all accusations of human misbehaviour ended.
There, guilty conscience was dealt with also by Jesus,
It was a place of crucifixion of all moral codes.
It was a place of getting saved by faith, not by Moses' Law.
No more will there be need for any other sacrifice to God.

At the cross God's infinite wisdom was demonstrated.
Christ's weakness in death gave way to eternal life.
God's wrath against sins was finally and totally paid for.
God's fulfilment of mankind's redemption promise was done.
Giving grace to those who believe in the death of His son.

INSPIRATIONS FOR THE MAN OF VALOUR

Only at the cross can you become completely free.
Free from that which has tormented you for so long.
Free from the yokes of sin, Satan, worry and fear.
Free from uncertainty and no fulfilment of the past and present.
Why delay any longer your meeting with Jesus at the Cross?[2]

---

[2] John 3:16; 1 Corinthians 1:20-25

# GOD'S LOVE LIKE THE SUN

God's love to mankind is just like the sun,
Always constant in position, timing and size,
Constant in intensity, never too hot or too cold,
Bright enough to penetrate through the clouds,
Shining on the wicked and the upright indiscriminately,
Reaching the poor and the rich no matter where,
Enjoyable by the young and the old people alike,
Giving life and health to every living thing,
Immeasurable by any man or any scientific means,
Can never be hidden by anything at anytime,
Can never be covered, concealed or denied,
Can always be received with childlike faith.

God's love has been given never to be withdrawn,
We all live by His love which gives us life,
Giving us enough strength and courage each day,
Searching us out amongst our sins and hopelessness,
Touching every part of our being, spiritual and physical,
Always available to every generation of mankind,
Reaching the deepest sea and highest mountain,
Melting every ice of uncertainty doubt and loss,
Banishing every darkness of despair and bondage,
Releasing every ingredient for growth in every way,
Bringing the best out of the worst of each sinner,
Breaking every racial and social barriers amongst recipients.[3]

3 Judges 5:31

# 2

## *Led by the spirit of God*

---

*My sheep hear my voice, and I know them, and they follow me:
And I give unto them eternal life; and they shall never perish,
neither shall any man pluck them out of my hand.*
*[John 10:27-28 (KJV)]*

*And thine ears shall hear a word behind thee, saying,
This is the way, walk ye in it,
when ye turn to the right hand,
and when ye turn to the left.*
*[Isaiah 30:21 (KJV)]*

## IT'S A MATTER OF WHERE YOU LOOK

Looking in the physical realm is very important to mankind,
For as we look we become appreciative of good scenery and people,
We may become repellent to what we consider to be disgusting or appalling,
Indeed no one old or young will voluntary want to be born or become blind.

Friend, it's a matter of just looking in that very circumstance,
For indeed looking reinforces every human belief and aspiration,
By how much you can clearly see is by the much you will receive,
Why not take God's own look this time in that very circumstance?

The promise of 'I will make you a father of Nations' was getting delayed,
Abraham and Sarah were aging with the biological set back of menopause,
The reality and shame of childlessness could no longer be hidden,
God's response to Abraham's petition and queries both times was just look!

Look up into the heavens and count the stars if you can God said,
Lift up now thine eyes and look from the place where thou art,
Northward and Southward, Eastward and Westward God said at another time,
For all the land which thou see, to thee I will give it and to thy seed forever.

In the survey of the Promised Land twelve spies were chosen to go and look,
All reported of the richness of the land, indeed a land with milk and honey,
Samples of figs and cluster of groups were brought for all to see,
Ten reported the city and the giant Anakin's compared to their small size.

The ten in their look could only see defeat awaiting their people,
They allowed their physical judgement to overrule their spiritual sight,
They forgot the miracles of God to them, starting from Egypt,
They allowed their faithless report to overrule that of Joshua and Caleb.

Their report influenced the emotional reactions of the 'people of God',
One thing led to another, fear, complaints, murmuring and rebellion,
None who was over twenty years except Joshua and Caleb was spared,
For they had allowed the ten spies' report to deflate their trust in the Lord.

Upon the death of Moses, it was time for Joshua to lead the Israelites,
God on occasions made Joshua to see the end result before the war started,
Reassuring him to see that every enemy was in fact, already defeated,
And walled cities were not difficult to capture once seen as already defeated.

Friend, it is time for you and I to take another look around us,
A look of forgiveness instead of punishment, peace instead of chaos,
A look of success instead of failure, prosperity instead of poverty,
For only as we have God's own look of the situation is victory guaranteed.[4]

---

[4] Genesis 15, Numbers 13, Joshua 6:2, 11:6.

## LOOKING AT THE OUTSIDE

We all have opportunities of making choices,
Some of our choices are not really that significant,
Others demand careful, thoughtful and prayerful steps,
For they will have a reasonable influence on our lives.

How do you go about making your choices?
Appearances many times can be deceitful,
Just as a pretty glaze covers a common clay pot,
Indeed not all that glitters is gold.

In choosing a king to replace disobedient Saul,
Samuel, the prophet had to visit Jesse and his family,
Whilst he assessed each son by their outside appearance,
God looked on the inside of the heart of each one of them.

Almost completely forgotten, youthful David was God's choice,
Though the smallest in age and in size,
He was finally chosen and anointed king by Prophet Samuel,
Little wonder he was called the man after God's own heart.

In the fight of Israel against the oppressing Philistines,
No one including tall, handsome King Saul could challenge Goliath,
Not enrolled in the army, David was busy keeping sheep,
His father's message to his brothers took him to the battle camp.

## INSPIRATIONS FOR THE MAN OF VALOUR

For the love of Jehovah, the Living God of Israel,
David challenged Goliath, without the typical soldier's apparel,
Too small by any human comparison for Goliath the giant,
Yet God granted Israel victory over the Philistine through him.

The outside look of weakness does not imply unreliability,
The outside look of ugliness does not mean lack of inner beauty,
The outside look of smallness does not imply lack of inner greatness,
The outside look of a simplicity does not mean lack of Godly wisdom.

The outside look of landmarks does not imply spiritual dead ends,
The outside look of dryness does not indicate lack of spiritual oasis,
The outside look of fragility does not imply lack of great spiritual strength,
Friend in your choices do not be carried away by the outside look.[5]

---

[5] 1Samuel 16:7

## YOUR APPROVAL IS REQUIRED

The Pharisees and the High Priest had a plan,
To get rid of Jesus through crucifixion,
They arrested him and at last their plan was fulfilled,
Yet they could not kill Him directly because the law forbade them,
They required the approval of the reigning Pilate.

Crucify Him, Crucify Him; that was the cry from the Pharisees and the High Priest
Judas had sold out his Master for only 30 pieces of silver,
At last we have Him where we want Him, they must have said within themselves,
Hey, not so fast, the law screamed loud and clear,
Remember, Pilate has to put his seal on this murder.

Haman in his enmity for Mordecai devised a wicked plan,
To get rid of Mordecai and all the Jews as well,
Although he was the Prime Minister, he could not go ahead with his plan,
He required the approval of Ahauserus, King of Persia and Medes.

Haman had a deep hatred for Mordecai because he just would not bow,
I know what to do, he thought within himself,
Build me a gallow eight cubits high, for Mordecai and all the Jews to hang,
Prime Minister although he was, his plan could not be brought to book
No, not before the King approved!

Honest, hardworking, faultless Daniel was hated by his colleagues,
They set a trap to find fault with him through his regular prayer sessions,
To the Lions' den the law demanded,
Yet they needed the approval of the King to carry out their wicked plans.

Pure, honest and prosperous Job was the target of the devil.
His faith in God was to be thoroughly tried and tested,
Yet at every stage of the devil's attack on innocent Job,
The Devil had to require the Almighty God's approval beforehand.

You too might be under the attack of the devil,
You might be the target of some wicked plots, unknowingly,
Remember in all of these God's approval is required,
For your life is hid in Christ and Christ's in God the Father.

God will not allow you to be tempted beyond your limits,
He will sustain you all through the fiery trials and temptations,
As you remain loyal and steadfast in faith in Him alone,
He will bring glory to His Name and blessings to you in all of it.

Are you in the corridor of power over the people or society?
Many of your subordinates will require your approval for one thing or another.
Be not unwearied as the King of Persia and Pilate in giving your approval,
For one day before the Almighty God,
You will have to account for all approvals given by you.

You do not have to succumb to the people's hasty demands.
In giving your approval be sure of the implications now and later.
Do not be carried off by your approval is required requests.
For the technicalities of your approval might mean hardship or death to many.[6]

[6] Mark 15:14; Matthew 18:18

# 3

## Watchfulness

*Be sober, be vigilant; because your adversary the devil, as a roaring lion, walketh about, seeking whom he may devour:*
*[1 Peter 5:8 (KJV)]*

*Give not sleep to thine eyes, nor slumber to thine eyelids. Deliver thyself as a roe from the hand of the hunter, and as a bird from the hand of the fowler.*
*[Proverbs 6:4-5 (KJV)]*

# KEEP AWAKE!

Keep awake and pray the Master said,
Lest temptations overpower you,
Indeed the spirit is willing,
But how weak the body is

Keep awake and pray the Master said,
Lest tribulations overpower you,
Indeed the sprit is willing,
But how weak the body is

Keep awake and pray the Master said,
Lest persecutions overpower you,
Indeed the spirit is willing,
But how weak the body is

Keep awake and pray the Master is saying,
Then victory is assured,
For greater is He that is in you,
Than they that are in the world.[7]

---

[7] Matthew 26:41 and 1 John 4:4

# FAMILY PLAN

God is interested in everyone, male or female,
In the old or young, rich or poor, whatever the race,
In the wise or foolish, in the literate or illiterate,
However, God is much more interested in families,
His blessings abide through obedience and curses through disobedience.

Adam and Eve were the ones that sinned in Eden,
The repercussion and punishment was to be on them,
Together with their generations yet unborn.
Noah was the only righteous man on earth in his time,
The Lord saved him together with all members of his household.

Abraham believed God and was counted righteous,
The promise of blessings for his faith was that his family
Would be made into a multitude of nations thereafter.
Lot was the only man found righteous in Sodom city,
He and his family were spared from the destruction.

Rahab the prostitute helped the spies at Jericho,
In return for her kind gesture she asked for a favour,
In addition to her life being spared, the spies promised
The safety of her family and those with her in her house,
What more? They all still live among the Israelites.

## INSPIRATIONS FOR THE MAN OF VALOUR

Achan the greedy man disobeyed Joshua's instruction,
He kept a beautiful robe, some silver and a bar of gold,
This made the Lord angry and the Israelites were defeated at Ai.
The punishment of stoning to death was not for him only,
But for his family who might have been unaware of his sin.

Short Zachaeus the notorious tax collector,
In a bid to see Jesus climbed the sycamore tree,
Jesus in love when He got to where Zachaeus was,
Beckoned to him to come down as he would be his guest.
That very day, salvation came to his whole house.

Cornelius a captain of an Italian regiment in Caesera,
Was a godly, reverent, generous man of prayer,
Noticed by God for his prayers and charity, an angel was sent to him,
To send for Peter, who lived with Simon the Tanner,
He and all that were with him were saved and Holy Ghost filled.

Paul and Silas miraculously released by an earthquake,
From prison whilst under the close watch of the jailer,
Waking up in the morning and finding the doors opened,
And the chains of every prisoner fallen off, the jailer ran,
To Paul and Silas asking them, "what shall I do to be saved?"

They replied 'believe on the Lord Jesus and you will be saved',
Together with your household they explained to him.
That same hour the jailer washed their wounds,
More importantly he and all his family believed them,
And confessing their faith in Jesus Christ they were all baptized.

For all children of God who are of age and irrespective of race,
Except the Holy Spirit of God has personally ministered otherwise,
For you to continue in the link of God's promises and blessings,
You must obey God by doing His will having your own family,
For the Almighty God's plan for man is a family plan.[8]

---

[8] Genesis 15:6; Joshua 6: 17 & 25 8:20-26; Luke 19: 1-10; Acts 10:1-4. 44-48 & 16:25-38

# COSTLY MISTAKE

Married at last to the beauty of my life
Inherited all of God's covenant promises
Along with all that my parents ever had
I certainly was the happiest man alive.

For many years we tried to have a child,
Remembered it took my parents sometime to have me,
Felt never mind, my wife and I will get there someday,
But year after year my wife became agitated and concerned.

In the heat of the pressures I sought the face of the Lord,
My father had taught me about His unfailing love and mercy,
I called on Him on behalf of my beautiful wife, lover and friend,
He answered and blessed us with the long-awaited pregnancy.

Now my wife will be very happy and enjoy this much-desired pregnancy,
But she was full of pains, aches and there was much struggling within her,
She sought the Lord and asked why she was in so much pains and aches,
Surprised, she was told in her were two people with different destinies.

At birth I loved Esau better than Jacob his brother, my favourite he became,
I could not but show my obvious preference of Esau over Jacob his brother,
I loved his hunting abilities and the meat he brought home from hunting,
I felt comfortable as Rebecca too made Jacob her favourite son over Esau.

Looking back now I realise that was a costly mistake by my wife and I,
Instead of fostering unity in my family it brought jealousy and untold anger,
A costly mistake we had made, which was obvious and late to correct,
A costly mistake that brought untold disunity and destruction in my family.

[9]Favouritism is a costly mistake that should be avoided in the family,
Learn to appreciate each other's uniqueness, abilities and strengths,
Endeavour to love each child equally and be fair to each one of them,
Favouritism is a costly mistake that we made, please learn from us.

---

[9] Genesis 25:19-34

# TRAIN THEM OR LOOSE THEM

I was the high priest for my generation,
I served God and His people,
As best as I knew, I served day and night,
Blessed with two sons, a happy man I was.

I thought they would follow in all my steps,
Fearing the Lord and serving Him and the people,
They knew all about the priestly procedures I felt,
Until I received reports of their brash behaviour.

A prophet came and warned me about my sons,
I called them and told them off for their bad actions,
Little Samuel also had a vision from God one night,
My boys after all were not as trained as I had thought.

Too late to train them I thought so I warned them,
I was too busy with God's assignment and the people,
I had little Samuel to bring up in the way of the Lord,
In the end I left the situation, not doing much to change it.

Train them or lose them I kept hearing over and over again,
How do I now train my matured, greedy and godless sons?
Then came an unexpected war with the Philistines our enemies,
In the same day both sons and a daughter in–law died.[10]

[10] 1 Samuel 3:10-21; 4:1-21

# I LOVED THEM BOTH DEARLY

Mine were the two boys, both from my loins,
The younger was somewhat lazy and inconsiderate,
Not too keen on the work on the farms,
Selfish often in his thinking and actions,
But I loved him dearly.

Once he came to make a request of me,
Of having his inheritance whilst I was alive,
He couldn't wait for me to pass on to glory,
Selfishly he demanded his right at the wrong time,
But I loved him still.

I gave him his inheritance and to a far country he went,
Not telling me where he was off to or for how long he would be gone,
Not minding what torments his request had on us,
To me, his mother, brother, family and friends,
But I loved him though.

I was heartbroken when he left,
I did not stop him from travelling even though I could,
I allowed him to go for a lifetime adventure,
I believed and prayed he would come back home,
But I loved him dearly.

Every day I watched out for his homecoming,
No one seemed to have a clue where he was,
No one told me what sort of life he was living,
No one but I kept on watching out for him,
But I loved him still.

One ordinary day I saw someone coming up our path,
Ragged, weary, worn out and in shame he came,
Apologising for his past mistakes to God and to me,
Asking that he be considered for a servant position,
But I loved him even more.

I embraced him in love and wept over him,
Prayers answered and dreams come to pass,
I ordered that he be clothed in new garments,
A ring for his finger and shoes for his weary feet,
Because I loved him still.

I ordered that the fattened calf be killed,
It was time for a huge family celebration,
My younger son's return was worth it all,
A time to publicly restore him to his sonship position,
Now I loved him best.

My older son very obedient and hardworking,
Unlike his brother never asking, hardly daring,
He was always by my side come rain come sunshine,
He was on the farm when his younger brother arrived,
I loved him very much too.

# INSPIRATIONS FOR THE MAN OF VALOUR

All these years he has been by my side working,
He had watched my character and attitude day and night,
I longed for him to at least be like me in his attitude,
Alas he refused to come into the party because of anger,
But I loved him too.

I went out to meet him and asked him why he was angry,
He told me I had never given him a kid to celebrate with his friends,
He judged his younger brother's lifestyle abroad without seeing him,
He seemed not to care whether his younger brother lived or died,
But I loved him more.

'All I have is yours son', I told him to his amazement,
You did not have because you did not ask me for anything,
The blood of the calf has been shed in the party for you and your brother,
The party is only for those who would come just as they were,
But I loved him too very much.

Mine were the two boys both from my loins,
Different in character, attitude and traits,
Same parents, same upbringing, same environment,
Different in what was in their minds and life goals,
But I loved them both and equally too.[11]

---

[11] Luke 15:11-32

# 4

## Consecration and intimacy with God

*I beseech you therefore, brethren, by the mercies of God,
that ye present your bodies a living sacrifice,
holy, acceptable unto God,
which is your reasonable service.
[Romans 12:1 (KJV)]*

*As the hart panteth after the water brooks,
so panteth my soul after thee, O God.
My soul thirsteth for God, for the living God:
when shall I come and appear before God?
[Psalms 42:1-3 (KJV)]*

# THY WILL BE DONE O LORD

When like precious Joseph I am being abandoned,
By those who are supposed to be very close to me,
Lord, help me to keep doing all the good I know unto others,
Looking forward to a breakthrough someday saying,
Thy will be done O Lord.

When like David at the war front against 'Goliath', I am prepared,
And I am being offered all physical, man-made weapons,
Lord, help me to remember that the arms of flesh will certainly fail,
With boldness only in Your word may I say,
Thy will be done O Lord.

When all hope has been lost like that of Jonah the Prophet,
And in the submarine of discomfort, problems and uncertainty I find myself,
Remind me of Your promise that You will make all things work for good,
And right there may I confidently say,
Thy will be done O Lord.

When I am seriously tempted to give up my faith,
In Your previous, precious revelations to me,
Dear Lord, remind me only of my past experiences and Your faithfulness,
With a heart full of gratitude may I say,
Thy will be done O Lord.

## INSPIRATIONS FOR THE MAN OF VALOUR

When I am fed up with my job and my environment,
And I feel rightly justified to do so,
Dear Lord, help me to remember how many souls You have blessed,
In the process of my stay, saying,
Thy will be done O Lord.

When my friends and family cannot understand me,
And I cannot explain what I am doing and why,
Lord help me to remember that You are still leading me,
Unto Your expected end and say,
Thy will be done O Lord.

When I am at the crossroad, unsure of what to do,
And the vision seems to tarry on and on,
Lord help me to remember Your ever present presence with me,
Communing with You and saying,
Thy will be done O Lord.

When I have to suffer for the sake of the precious gospel,
And in the eyes of people I become a laughing stock,
Remind me of Jesus Christ's experience on the cross,
Boldly bearing the suffering and saying,
Thy will be done O Lord.

When You ask me to do certain things,
Things that are contrary to my own taste and nature,
Lord remind me that Your ways are not my ways,
Obediently and willingly may I say,
Thy will be done O Lord.

## INSPIRATIONS FOR THE MAN OF VALOUR

When I have to give up things that are precious to me,
Starting all over again in a new unknown environment,
Missing all my good old friends, colleagues and loving neighbours,
Thankful unto Thee may I say,
Thy will be done O Lord.[12]

---

[12] Luke 22:42

# ALONE WITH GOD

Many of us want to hear from God,
To listen to His small still voice,
Yet we never provide such an atmosphere,
And might not be quiet in our spirit,
To get directives and instructions from God.

Jacob, frightened to meet Esau,
On his way back home as directed by God,
With two armies and many flock,
Got assurance from God after wrestling with the angel,
While alone on the other side of River Jordan.

Great men and women in the Bible,
Became great for they heard from God,
Whilst they were alone with Him,
They found time out of none to be with Him,
In prayers and the study of His Word.

Many of us complain of our busy schedule,
For some it's their children or their family or wealth,
Whilst for others it's their many responsibilities,
Even when alone in their closets at home,
Their minds are not quietened to hear God.

Alone with God my brother,
Get your spirit off your family and associates,
Off your many duties and responsibilities,
In the closet of your heart talk with God,
In prayers and meditation on God's Words.

Time spent alone with God in your closet,
Is time better spent than any other time,
For not only will you be re-assured,
Comforted, encouraged and nurtured,
It is a time of receiving clear directives from God.

Take time to be alone with God my brother, my friend,
Wherever you are now and whatever you may be doing,
God is ready to give you directives on your problems,
For 'in returning and rest you shall be saved,
In quietness and in trust shall be your strength'.[13]

---

[13] Genesis 22:9-12, 22-32 & Isaiah 30:15.

# I'D LOVE TO SEE MY SAVIOUR

I'd love to see my Saviour,
I'd love to be in His presence,
Just to confess my many sins,
His pardon and mercy to receive.

I'd love to see my Saviour,
I'd love to tell Him all my hurts,
I'd love to tell Him my troubles,
His victory and grace to receive.

I'd love to see my Saviour,
I'd love to experience His touch,
Healing every sickness and disability,
Delivered from every oppression.

I'd love to see my Saviour,
I'd love to hear Him speak to me,
Just to be in His presence,
His plans and instructions to receive.

I'd love to see my Saviour,
I'd love to be in His presence,
I'd love to worship Him only,
I'd love to see my Jesus today.[14]

---

[14] John 12:21

## ISAAC MUST GO

Many people have things that make them happy,
For some they have people who bring them laughter,
No matter what condition they are passing through,
The thought of that which they hold very dearly,
Or the presence of that person makes them happy.

For some it is their husbands or their children,
For others their wives, brothers, sisters, parents or friends,
For some it is their highly esteemed paying job,
For some it is their wealth, beauty of achievements,
Whilst for some, it is their enviable, comfortable position.

God gives, gives and gives us the best in life,
Such that He gave His only begotten son,
To die on the cross of Calvary just for you and I,
Dear friend, is anything too much for you to give Him
For all His manifold blessings upon you too many to count?.

Isaac, the promised child of the multimillionaire Abraham,
Was born under a faith-testing and approving circumstances,
No wonder he was named Isaac meaning laughter,
Whilst the joy of the parents and their friends knew no bounds,
He, Isaac had the best of everything he ever wanted.

Isaac was so precious to Father Abraham and Mother Sarah,
Yet God asked that Isaac be sacrificed unto Him,
Abraham had to obediently yield Isaac on the altar,
For the Lord wanted the best and most treasured for Himself,
Though very difficult, Abraham obeyed God and was rewarded.

Every material thing will pass away dearest friend,
That untouchable precious Isaac must go dear friend,
Whether it be that ambition, job, desire or wealth,
Be it your husband, wife, relatives, children or friends,
Though very precious to you, it must be sacrificed.

That Isaac must go, I repeat, dear friend,
*It must be laid on the altar of God for sacrifice,
Give it up to your God and be ready to live victoriously,
For it is in your giving that Isaac that you stand to be blessed,
Time to obey dear friend that Isaac must go.[15]

---

* Put God first above everything that you hold in highest esteem. The poem does not imply the reader killing anyone.

[15] Genesis 22:2

# TAKE TIME

Take time to admire,
God's richness in every creature He made around,
Though little and insignificant,
Yet every creature speaks volumes
Of God's beauty and wisdom.

Take time to fellowship,
For there, Christ's presence you will experience,
Sharing the word and bread with others,
Becoming a blessing to others,
As you too are richly blessed.

Take time to listen,
Best communicators are very good at listening,
Listen to the needs around,
And what's more?
To the silent still voice of the Holy Spirit.

Take time to love,
For that is the nature of our Father in heaven,
Costly as it may be some times,
It is the only thing that will remain
After all other things and gifts cease.

Take time to listen,
Listen to the people around you,
Listen to their spoken words,
And to their unspoken but
Expressed challenges and fear.

Take time to pray,
For in it lies divine power and revelation,
Christ is our unique example,
And a prayer-less Christian,
Is a powerless one.

Take time to read God's word,
For it is a lamp to your feet and light to your path,
A never failing compass,
Which directs you rightly
Through this earthly pilgrimage to heaven.

Take time to read God's word,
For in it God's plans and purposes are revealed,
An answer to every problem you will find,
A successful guide through life,
You will experience.

Take time to reflect,
On God's answer to your prayers and the many blessings,
Refreshing and reassuring,
Your courage renewed and
Faith strengthened for the future.

## INSPIRATIONS FOR THE MAN OF VALOUR

Take time to serve,
For in that lowly service lies true and good leadership,
And what's more?
There is a great reward
For all your humble service.

Take time to share the gospel,
For that is the only assignment Christ gave to believers,
As He ascended heaven,
And each addition to the fold,
Causes great rejoicing in heaven.

Take time to sing,
For even birds use their voices in praising God,
And as you sing,
You invoke the presence of the Holy Spirit.

Take time to sing,
For it is the only occupation there in heaven,
A good practice here,
Gives a foretaste,
Of eternity yet to come.

Take time to visit others,
For in judgment you will be rewarded,
And whilst you are away,
Devil cannot meet you at home,
To tempt, use or destroy you.

Take time to write,
Encouraging others in this earthly pilgrimage,
And when you are no more,
It will be a legacy to,
Many generations to come.

Take time today beloved,
Amidst your busy schedule,
Go out of your way,
Do that which for so long,
You have neglected in your Christian life.[16]

---

[16] E Ecclesiastes 3:1-9

# OPEN LORD

Open my eyes Lord,
That I might see Jesus.

Open my ears Lord,
That I might hear Jesus.

Open my heart Lord,
That I might receive Him.

Open my mouth Lord,
That I might sing unto Him.

Open my hands Lord,
That I might touch His garment.

Open my life Lord,
That I might obey Him.

Open my being Lord,
That I might serve Him forever. (Amen)[17]

---

[17] Ephesians 1:15-19

# 5

## Faith in God

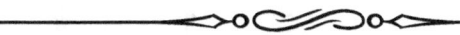

*But without faith it is impossible to please Him:
for He that cometh to God must believe that He is,
and that He is a rewarder of them that diligently
seek Him.
[Hebrew 11:6 (KJV)]*

*But that no man is justified by the law in the
sight of God,
it is evident: for, The just shall live by faith.
[Galatians 3:11 (KJV)]*

# AS A MAN THINKS

As a man thinks so he is, goes the saying,
What is the size of your God?
What is the limit of the Glory of your God?
What are the limitations of His power, presence and personality?
Who is He to you each time?

When you think about the Almighty God,
What sort of thoughts do you have about Him?
What sort of image do you have in your mind?
What sort of limitations do you attribute to Him?
What sort of inspiration do you receive from Him?

As a man thinks of His God so he receives,
Your ability to receive great and mighty gifts,
Your ability to continually be in His presence,
Your privilege to remain in fellowship,
All depends on who your God is.

If you think your God is very small,
Then you should be contented with small things,
If you think your God is very, very big,
Then you will agree that nothing is bigger than Him,
No matter what the problem or circumstance might be.

Many of us have ignorantly complained about God,
When we have been the main cause of our problems,
We accuse Him of things He will not do,
We leave Him out of minor and major decisions,
And we limit our God's power, purpose and prerogatives.

Friend, your thinking has affected you thus far,
Such that you are full of many negative thoughts,
No wonder you don't get anything done and on time,
Such that your confessions are depressing and sad,
No wonder you have lived a miserable, unproductive life.

Why will you continue to think negatively and small?
Why will you refuse God's gift of possible intervention?
Why will you remain carnal in your thinking?
Why refuse to broaden your imagination of God?
Why continue to focus your thinking on your circumstances?

As a man thinks so he really is.
If you will humbly ask God to help you brother,
To create in you a new clean heart today,
Filled with clean thoughts and right desires,
Then will your mountain of problems be levelled.

As a man thinks so he is.
You no longer have any sincere excuse,
Not to possess your possession right away,
Will you today reconsider your moment-by-moment thoughts,
For indeed as a man thinks so he really is.[18]

---

[18] Proverbs 23:7

## AT LIFE'S EDGE

Failure in life sometimes is not limited to the weak and unprepared,
Experienced, prepared and brilliant people sometimes fail too,
In spite of their hard work, experience, abilities and intelligence,
It must be so painful and stressful not to have anything to show for it.

Simon Peter and his friends had been fishing all through the night,
They were professional fishermen who understood their trade,
They toiled all night in the dark and coldness on the sea,
They caught nothing by morning; what a wasted effort!

At the edge of the waters stood their boats as they mended their nets,
In their tiredness and weariness they prepared for the next day,
Close by on the seashore a great crowd had gathered and possibly watching,
For Jesus was there preaching on the shore of that very lake.

They must have been disappointed and frustrated by their failure,
At the water's edge stood their boats that were empty,
They were engrossed in the washing and mending of their nets,
Joining the crowd to listen to Jesus was not for them at that moment.

Noticing the two empty boats at the edge of the water,
Jesus stepped into one of them and asked Simon the owner for a push,
Out a little into the waters so He could sit in it and preach to the crowd,
Who had been earlier pressing on Him to hear the Word of God.

Perhaps today you are at life's edge, frustrated by your failure,
Your boats are empty, you are washing and mending your professional tools,
You have nothing to show for your hard work and midnight toils,
And what's more? There is a great crowd around possibly watching.

At life's edge of problems and failures you are standing,
Your experience, expertise, formulas and input have failed you,
You are exhausted, tired and possibly fed up with everything,
Friend, don't despair as God is about to bring about your miracle.

You are possibly too engrossed in your failures, tired and weary,
Another stress could possibly give you a complete breakdown,
Too sad to join the crowds whatever the cause of their gathering,
Too busy mending and minding your own business and life.

Jesus is there, right there at your life's edge brother and friend,
You are so special that He wants to come right into your situation,
Not only to sort you out but equally to use and bless you,
To fill your empty boat to overflowing, dear friend.

At life's edge God is going to meet you and speak to you,
A response to His demand He will expect from you,
A change beyond your expectation and understanding will occur,
Failures will be turned to fruitfulness as you faithfully obey Him.

As He calls you out from the midst of the crowd,
Not only to get your attention but to ask for that empty boat,
Asking you once again to try in that in which you once have failed,
Not to ridicule you in front of the crowd but to bless you abundantly so.[19]

[19] Luke.5:1-11

# BUT WHOSE REPORT WILL YOU BELIEVE?

At last the Doctors have come up with your diagnosis
They have come up with the prognosis of what to expect from now
The pains they say will never go away, the wounds won't heal
The condition they say may likely get worse from now on
But whose report will you believe?

The bank statement is here again in the usual envelope
The account is not only red but very red with overdrawn overdraft
The end of the tax year has come and your can't balance your books
The creditors are at your tail with a threat of visit from the debt collector
But whose report will you believe?

The marriage is not over but it seems and feels well over
Communication between both of you is rather very sore
Commitment to make it work has lost its zeal and ability
Concern for each other's welfare is certainly lacking and obvious
But whose report will you believe?

The treasured job is over when you have least expected
There is no other job in site to keep you busy and thinking
There is your age and possibly your lack of much education
There is your family and other responsibilities to be concerned about
But whose report will you believe?

## INSPIRATIONS FOR THE MAN OF VALOUR

The situation you are in is very real dear friend
There is no running away from the obvious facts
There is no known human solution in site
There is no man who could solve that problem
But whose report will you believe?

Time now to accept the facts as they lay before you
Time now to hand these facts to your Maker and Lord
Time now to seek for the truth about your situation in the Bible
Time now to turn your focus only on the truth as written in the Bible
Facts or truth the choice of your belief will determine the outcome

God's truth will any day override man's fact
For He speaks no careless word to anyone
His words are true, pure and sure to anyone who believes
He backs His words by His name and Himself
Facts or truth whose report will you believe?[20]

---

[20] Isaiah 53:1; Matthew 16:13-16

## CASTING ALL UPON HIM

There is no human being without a problem
The problems are of various types and severity
Why will you continue to be bear these problems?
When you can safely cast all upon the Lord.

The more you hide that particular problem of yours,
The bigger it will certainly become from experience,
Why will you not share it today with the Saviour?
Who is anxiously and willingly ready to solve it for you?

Moses was born at a time when the decree forbade male children,
Being an unusually beautiful baby his mother hid him at home
What should have been a natural source of joy and happiness
Became a big problem and burden to the family of Moses.

His mother out of love, hid him for three months after birth,
However Moses was getting bigger with stronger voice,
When she could no longer hide him because of the decree,
She made a basket from papyrus reed, water-proofed with tar.

She put him in the basket boat along the river edge
She left him there and returned to her home
Possibly without any hope of seeing her child again
Or possibly hoping in her God for a miraculous intervention.

## INSPIRATIONS FOR THE MAN OF VALOUR

God in His infinite plan and love for the Israelites
Saved Moses' life through one of Pharaoh's daughters
Not only this, he was given to his biological mother to nurse
He grew up trained as one of Pharaoh's grandsons.

If you will today believe in the infinite power of God,
And will openly cast all your cares and burdens upon Him,
Completely leaving them at the foot of the cross of Calvary,
You will experience the Divine intervention and solution from God.[21]

---

[21] Exodus.2:1-10

# I WILL LIFT UP MY EYES
## (Psalm 121)

*I will lift up my eyes to the mountains;*
*from whence shall my help come?*
Lord, when I look at the mountains,
They seem way high up above,
Solid, strong and immovable,
Yet my help cannot come from the mountains,
For they are themselves without life.

*My help comes from the Lord,*
*who made heaven and earth.*
Lord, in times past, my help has come from You,
Maker of heaven and earth,
Even though You are my Father and Lord,
By creative and redemptive rights,
Yet it seems You are so far away from me at the moment,
And my cries to You for help appear unanswered,
But if You would help me Lord,
None of Your creatures can stand in my way of progress,
Therefore Lord I need Your help against my adversaries and oppressors,
Who for the fact that You tarry,
Appear to me, way high up like the mountains.

## INSPIRATIONS FOR THE MAN OF VALOUR

*He will not allow my foot to slip,*
*He who keeps me will not slumber.*
Behold He who keeps Israel will neither slumber nor sleep.
Lord, these words express how vulnerable I am without Your help,
These days I cannot feel You holding my hands,
And I fear that my foot is about to slip.
Much as I believe that You neither sleep nor slumber,
To lose Your grip on me,
Yet I do not feel Your hold as before,
And as a child I am frightened,
And feel completely alone and abandoned.

*The Lord is my keeper. The Lord is my shade on my right.*
*The Sun will not smite me by day nor the moon by night.*
Thank You Lord for being my keeper,
You have been my protector in times past.
Come once again and be a shade for me,
From the surrounding heat of oppression,
Injustice, wickedness, poverty, failure, loss and loneliness,
So that I might not be smitten by them in Jesus' name.

*The Lord will protect me from all evil. He will keep my soul.*
Lord protect me according to Your promise,
From all forms of evil including unbelief and pride,
Which may want to attack my soul,
At this time of great need,
And keep my soul from denying You.

INSPIRATIONS FOR THE MAN OF VALOUR

***The Lord will guard my going in and coming out from this time forth and ever more.***
Thank You Lord for the promise,
Of guarding my ways and being with me forever.
As I go daily about my duties and tasks,
May I experience Your leading and protection,
Once more and always in Jesus name. (Amen.)[22]

---

[22] Psalm 121

# LOOKING UP TO HEAVEN

Shall I look to the mountain gods for help?
No! My help is from Jehovah who made the mountains,
He made the heavens, the earth and their contents,
He made man in His very own image.

At the tomb of Lazarus four days after his death,
Jesus looked up to heaven after weeping,
Thanking God He shouted; "Lazarus, come out"
Immediately Lazarus came out of the tomb.

A deaf man with a speech impediment,
Was brought to Jesus to be healed,
Looking up to heaven he sighed and commanded,
"Open!", immediately the man could hear and speak.

About five thousand people not counting women and children,
Were hungry after listening to Jesus' teaching,
Looking around the disciples could only get,
Five loaves of bread and two fishes from a boy.

Jesus commanded the people to sit on the grass,
In fifties and hundreds the disciples sat them,
Looking up to heaven, He blessed the food,
They were all well fed and there were leftovers.

INSPIRATIONS FOR THE MAN OF VALOUR

Looking up to heaven focuses our attention on to God,
From whom all blessings and powers flow,
We are no longer distracted by the problems or circumstances,
But we become conduit pipes for the flow of the Holy Spirit.[23]

[23] Psalms 21: 1-2, John11:35, Mark 7:34; Mark 6:35-42

# 6

## His call

---

*I press toward the mark for the prize of the high calling of God in Christ Jesus.*
*[Phil 3:14 (KJV)]*

*Be not thou therefore ashamed of the testimony of our Lord, nor of me His prisoner: but be thou partaker of the afflictions of the gospel according to the power of God;*
*Who hath saved us, and called us with an holy calling,*
*not according to our works, but according to His own purpose and grace,*
*which was given us in Christ Jesus before the world began,*
*[2 Tim 1:8-9 (KJV)]*

INSPIRATIONS FOR THE MAN OF VALOUR

# WHAT IS YOUR CALLING?

For every child of God there is a calling,
An area which God has entrusted to you.
But how many today know their calling?
And if they do, how many are faithful in it?

Adam was to tend the Garden of Eden.
Abraham's was the possession of a land which God would show him.
Joseph was to administer the world economy during famine.

Moses' was leading Israel out of Egypt to the Promised Land.
For David his was the Kingdom of Israel to rule,
For Joshua his was entering and conquering the Promised Land.

For Daniel, it was an unquestioned rule in Babylon.
And Solomon, it was building the temple of God.
Samson was to deliver his people from the Philistines,

Caleb's was the bringing of good reports.
Jesus' calling was the salvation and redemption of mankind,
While Peter's was to be an apostle to the Jews.

For the disciples theirs was the preaching of the Good News,
For Abigail hers was intercession for her household.
For Deborah hers was judging the people and leading them into battle,

## INSPIRATIONS FOR THE MAN OF VALOUR

For Rahab hers was the outreach to the two Israelite spies.
Jeremiah was called to warn the Nations,
And the Levites were to serve at the temple.

Brother, what is your calling?
And how faithful have you been to it?
Perhaps it's time to re-access your performance?
Or time to ask God for greater anointing upon your call?

God has a calling for you, dear brother,
A purpose in this world which only you can meet.
The list is inexhaustible for all I know,
Where is your place in His ministry to mankind?[24]

---

[24] 1 Corinthians 7:20

# HE MAKES US GO

God in his infinite love, mercies and plan for mankind,
Has ordained that specific people do specific things for mankind,
According to His plans at specific times He calls them out,
What a shame as many who are called many times often refuse?

Such was the case of Moses when he was on Mount Sinai,
Tending his father in laws flock all alone, God called him.
Five times he pleaded that God might seek someone else,
Rather than agree five times he gave different excuses to God,
But the Lord had made His choice and Moses must go,
This will not make God change His mind for Moses had to go.

Jonah the son of Amittaic was sent by God to great Nineveh,
In fear he thought he could run away from the Almighty God,
To a land farther away from Nineveh, aboard a ship to Tarshish,
Running away from God he boarded a ship going to Tarshish.
His peace he found in surrender to God's will as he returned in a fish's belly.
He accepted God's instruction and went to Nineveh after the fish spit him out.

The Angel of the Lord visited Gideon with a heavenly message.
That God had appointed him to deliver the Israelites from the Midianites.
Rather than being happy and bold for that assignment beloved.
Gideon started giving excuses but in the end God made him to go.

Peter in a trance at Simon the tanner's house was offered food thrice.
With a heavenly voice telling him to go on, kill and eat.
Thrice he refused to obey God and the sheet was lifted to heaven.
He awoke to find Cornelius messengers looking for him and he had to go.

Beloved, the Lord has called you and you have heard.
Your excuse could be that you have a physical defect like Moses.
Or yours could be that you are very afraid of God like Jonah.
Or yours could be that you are from an insignificant family like Gideon.

Friend, God might be asking you to do something contrary to your taste.
His offer to you might be like the food offer to Peter in a trance.
Whatever your excuse might be, this cannot change God's eternal plan.
He will make you go in the end so why continue to give those excuses?[25]

---

[25] Exodus 3:4; Jonah 1:2; Judges 6:11:16; Acts 10:1-28.

# CAN HE USE YOU?

God has a purpose for every life He created,
No matter the hardships or handicaps of a person,
No matter the sinful and purposeless life of a person,
No matter what others think about him,
No matter the subjective and societal condemnation of him.

To lead over six hundred thousand people out of the Egyptians' bondage,
God's choice of a leader was Moses the stammerer,
To lead the church after Jesus' death,
Jesus' choice was a shaking reed like Peter, the fisherman.

To feed the prophet throughout the years of famine,
God's choice was the poor widow with the last meal,
To host Prophet Elisha during his frequent stopovers,
God's choice was the childless Shunamite woman.

To save Israel from the hand of the wicked Midianites,
God's choice was Gideon, from the least tribe and poorest family,
To save mankind from sin and death, God's choice was Jesus,
"the son of the Carpenter".

For information on how best to capture fortified city of Jericho,
God's choice was Rahab the well-known prostitute,
To be the first woman evangelist in the Samaritan town,
Jesus' choice was the unnamed, unmarried prostitute.

# INSPIRATIONS FOR THE MAN OF VALOUR

For replacing disobedient Israel's first king Saul,
God's choice was little David, the shepherd boy from the field,
For replacing Judas Iscariot who betrayed Jesus Christ,
God's choice among others was the man named Matthias.

To see first the glorious risen Saviour on Easter morning,
God's choice was Mary from whom seven demons has been cast out.
To bring the good news of God's destruction of the Syrian army,
God's choice was the despised, unwanted, unnamed four lepers.

To publicly and boldly preach Jesus Christ as a prophet of God,
God's choice was the man born blind and who for long had been beggar.
To preach Jesus as Lord in the town that rejected him,
Jesus choice was the possessed demonic man whom He healed.

God's choice for that seemingly difficult assignment is you,
You can be used for that seemingly difficult assignment,
For God's choice of the person He is looking for is you.
Irrespective of your handicap, previous sinful life and social stigma,
For God's Glory comes out best in weak and feeble vessels like you.[26]

---

[26] 2 Timothy 2:20

# IDENTIFICATION SEAL

God has endowed each one with their specific identification,
This ranges from our name, personality to our achievements,
Sometimes too it may be our possessions and wealth,
Each person having his/her own identification seal.

For Esau it was his God-given birth right and blessings,
Which for a plate of porridge he traded with Jacob,
The consequences of which was a great, lifelong loss,
As God's covenant to Abraham passed on to Jacob instead of him.

For Joseph, his identification was his coat of many colours,
Which he lost to his jealous brothers when he was sold by them,
Later at Potiphar's house, it was his jacket yet again,
Which he lost to the lustful, unfaithful wife of Potiphar.

For Judah the unknown prostitute demanded his identification seal,
Which he gave to her and his walking stick before their love-making,
Thereafter he couldn't get it back as she was untraceable,
The result of which became a thing of shame to Judah.

For Job, his enormous wealth, children, and cattle, identified him,
All of which unfortunately, he lost within hours,
He equally lost his health to uncountable painful boils,
Such that his visiting friends who heard could not recognize him.

Friend, have you stopped to think of your identification seal?
It could be your health, personality, job, or family,
It could even be your position, beauty or good will,
Be careful for the devil watches to snatch away your identification seal.

For whatever reasons you might have lost your identification,
Be assured the Almighty God is able to return or replace it for you,
In Christ all things have passed away making everything new,
In Him alone do you stand anew with a new identification seal.[27]

---

[27] John 3:33; Galatians 6:17

# THE MAN CALLED JOSEPH

His mother's name was Rachael,
His father's name was Jacob,
The son of Isaac and Rebekah,
The son of Abraham and Sarah.

His brother's name was Benjamin,
He had ten other half brothers,
Who hated him so much,
They sold him away in slavery.

At the age of seventeen years,
He entered the services of Potiphar,
Even there the Lord blessed him,
And he became the administrator.

Though Potiphar's wife lured him,
Several times into an ungodly act,
He refused to listen to her request,
And kept out of her way always.

Unfortunately while alone at home,
Potiphar's wife tricked him again,
Leaving his jacket behind he ran,
And that landed him in prison.

There in the prison Joseph was,
Enjoying God's kindness and favour,
He became the prison administrator,
And the Lord was with him.

He being a considerate, loving person,
Asked the baker and the waiter their problems,
Giving glory to God alone,
He was able to interpret their dreams.

In the jail he was almost forgotten,
Until Pharaoh had two unresolved dreams,
Giving glory once again to God,
He told Pharaoh their meanings.

From a slave and a prisoner,
God elevated him to Egypt's administrator,
He became the second in command,
At the appointed time of the Lord.

Joseph filled with the spirit of God,
Did not revenge what his brothers did,
Rather he forgave and showed them love,
And gave them the best of all Egypt had.[28]

---

[28] Genesis 30:24 – 50:26

# 7

## *The all-sufficient and benevolent God*

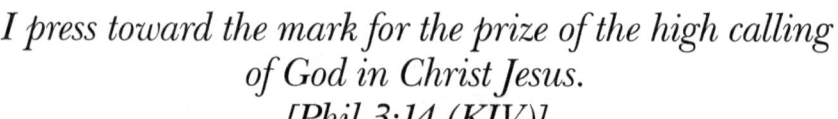

*I press toward the mark for the prize of the high calling of God in Christ Jesus.*
*[Phil 3:14 (KJV)]*

*Be not thou therefore ashamed of the testimony of our Lord, nor of me His prisoner: but be thou partaker of the afflictions of the gospel according to the power of God;*
*Who hath saved us, and called us with an holy calling, not according to our works, but according to his own purpose and grace, which was given us in Christ Jesus before the world began,*
*[2 Tim 1:8-9 (KJV)]*

## THE CAFETERIA

Cafeterias provide food,
Various dishes for various meals,
Some are spicy; others mild,
Some are sweet, others sour,
Cold drinks or hot, vegetables or fruits.

Some dishes take long to prepare or cook,
Others a few minutes or perhaps seconds,
Some dishes look really attractive and tempting,
Other dishes simply look plain and uninviting.

Some dishes are made for certain groups of people:
Vegetarians who don't eat animal products,
The diabetic or others on special diets,
Children with taste buds different from adults'.

Sweet or sour, we eat the dishes all,
To make us grow healthy and strong,
This is the lesson on faith, love and hope,
Partaking of the dishes makes us Christ-like and useful.

Man has the tendency to be hungry for food.
As well as thirsty for a drink; hot or cold,
While some live to eat most of their lives,
Others eat to live and face life's challenges.

At meal times the cafeteria trolleys are fully stocked.
Some cafeterias offer complete self-service
In some, orders are placed with the stewards,
Yet in others, there is minimal choice.

Sometimes Stewards stand behind the food trolleys
Waiting on diners and refilling the food trolleys when empty,
Giving a helping hand in serving customers,
Others stand behind the cash till to give the bill
and receive payment for the meal.

God has His cafeteria for the world; the Bible it is called,
With enough food for the hungry and drink for the thirsty
Every human spiritual need is already catered for,
It meets the desire of every age group and need.

The word of God is there at all times, in all seasons,
The Psalms for encouragement, Proverbs for wisdom,
Genesis for the creation story and Revelations for the latter days,
The Gospels for salvation and Jesus' ministry
The Epistles for nurturing, rebuke and encouragement.

Friend, what dish are you having at your next meal?
In the earthly cafeteria we pay for our choice,
In God's cafeteria, Christ has paid for all,
By His death on the cross, and by whose stripes we are healed.

Heavenly hosts wait on us at meal times,
Christ on God's right hand always interceding on our behalf,
Angels waiting upon us for our orders in God
How often do you visit God's cafeteria for mankind?[29]

---

[29] Jeremiah 31:25.

INSPIRATIONS FOR THE MAN OF VALOUR

# GOD'S PROVISION - My Part

God has enough provision for all the people in the world,
Who will dare to call upon Him for help with their needs.
In His storehouse, there is abundance for despatch,
But each one with a need has a part to play in receiving.

In the Garden of Eden, there was an abundance of food,
Fruits, vegetables, fishes and all types of animal meat,
But Adam and Eve had to choose what they wanted to eat,
As well as go and get it for themselves whenever they wanted.

The manna and quails, God provided for the Israelites,
Without failing for forty years on their way to the land of Canaan,
Daily except the Sabbath they had to go 'collecting their meals',
Manna flakes in the morning and quails in the evening.

The widow with her two sons were in great financial distress,
Unknown to them the jar of oil was God's provision,
They were to borrow as many pots and barrels from neighbours,
By faith behind closed doors, poured the jar of oil into the vessels.

Another widow with her son were preparing for their very last meal,
The famine was very severe with no hope for the next day,
Elijah the prophet demanded that he be served first,
And that was the beginning of a feeding programme for them.

## INSPIRATIONS FOR THE MAN OF VALOUR

For Peter and Jesus unable to pay their taxes when asked,
Peter was instructed to go and fish in the sea,
The first fish caught would have money in its mouth,
Enough to pay for Jesus' and Peter's taxes as demanded.

God has promised to meet that need my brother, my sister,
His part for providing for your needs He would fulfil,
My part and your part in receiving would require total obedience,
To God's instructions as He would graciously reveal.

My part, your part, my friend in meeting that need,
Requires us to identify and accept that we indeed have a need,
A need that only God can meet and He is willing to meet,
Trusting in His abundant provision and obedience to His leading. [30]

---

30 1 Kings 17:3-4; 17:9; Matthew 17:24-27

INSPIRATIONS FOR THE MAN OF VALOUR

# JESUS HAS THE POWER

Jesus has the power,
To speak life to the lifeless,
To replace any dead cell in your body,
To cast out demons from the oppressed,
To heal that sickness and make you whole.

Jesus has the power,
To make the impossible possible,
To provide water from the rock,
To provide all things from nothing,
To speak into existence things that are not.

Jesus has the power,
To save the lost sinner,
To set you free from those yokes,
To raise up the down-trodden,
To give hope to the hopeless.

Jesus has the power,
To give children to the barren,
To be parents to the orphans,
To prosper that which had not been prospering,
To make a way in the wilderness of life.

INSPIRATIONS FOR THE MAN OF VALOUR

**Jesus has the Super power,
To provide for every need of yours,
To change you and your lifestyle,
To roll away the stone of problems in your life,
To give you a future and bring you to an expected end.[31]**

---

[31] Matthew 28:18, Jeremiah 29:11

# MY UNLIMITED GOD

**PART 1**
My God is unlimited in every way and at every time,
How wonderful and marvellous He is in His dealings with mankind,
How faithful as He shows His love over and over again to us,
How timely are His interventions and accurate His judgements?

Imagine His unlimited wisdom displayed in every known creation of His,
Imagine the vast knowledge awaiting human discovery in every bit of life,
Imagine the beauty, protection, and provision for all living things,
Imagine the complexity, uniqueness and wonders in every life reproduced.

Think about His forgiveness to man whose heart and intent is constantly wicked ,
Think about His pardon of sin, no matter how grievous, at confession,
Think about His restoration and love to all – His prodigal children,
Think about His cleansing that leaves the sinner spotless and clean.

Remember His unlimited ways of speaking to His own, His elect and anointed,
Remember His revelations in dreams to Jacob, Joseph, Pharaoh and Daniel,
Remember His calling of Moses, Saul the King, Saul of Tarsus and Simon Peter,
Remember His visit to Abraham, Manoah's wife, Gideon and Mary, Jesus' mother.

## PART 2

Remember His unique ways of healing every disease encountered:
Healing of King Hezekiah by using a paste made from dried figs,
Healing of the paralytic man by the spoken word of Christ the Messiah,
Healing of Naaman the leper by seven immersions in the River Jordan.

Healing of the man born blind by applying mud to his eyes,
Healing of the unrestrained man by casting out the demons,
Healing of the centurion's servant by the word of command believed;
Healing of the woman with the issue of blood just by her touch of faith.

Healing of the Israelites of snake bites by looking up at the bronze serpent,
Healing of Abimelech's household of infertility by Abraham's prayer,
Healing of the water causing miscarriages by Elisha adding salt,
Healing from the poisoned meal by putting some of it back into the pot.

Provision of forty years food for the Israelites has never been equalled,
Provision of food to starving Elijah by the brook, through the ravens,
Provision of food for the widow and her son, through Elijah's words,
Provision of better wine at the wedding from water, very unique.

Leading of the Israelites to the Promised Land, by His presence,
Leading of the wise men to the promised Child, by the lone bright star,
Leading of the disciples to their assigned duties, by the Holy Spirit,
Leading of His children now, by the Scriptures and the Holy Spirit.

The salvation of Zacchaeus' family, by Jesus' invitation to Zacchaeus,
The salvation of the jailer's family, by his encounter with Paul and Silas,
The salvation of Cornelius's family, by the invitation of Simon Peter,
And our salvation, by confession and acceptance of His love by faith.

The final confirmation of a child to Abraham was during the three men's visit,
The deliverance of Lot and his family, by Lot's kindness to the two strangers,
The deliverance of the harlot and her family, by her kindness to the two spies,
The deliverance of mankind from Satan, sin and death is by Christ's redemption.

The surgical provision of a wife to Adam, incredibly remarkable,
The faithful way He led Abraham's servant to choose Rebecca, miraculous,
The beginning of the marital relations between Jacob and Rachel, unique,
The leading of Moses to meet his future bride at a well, amazing.

## PART 3
My unlimited God is capable of handling every situation, however hard!
He is capable of fighting on your behalf, without you fighting at all,
He is capable of bounteous provision no matter your need or want,
He is capable of restoring all that you have lost.

My unlimited God is Father, Saviour, Friend and Helper,
He is undemanding; not like any of the gods you have heard of anywhere,
He is unselective in His love and mercies toward mankind, no matter their colour,
He is easily approachable - anytime, anywhere and with any request.

My unlimited God is caring- He knows each of His own by name,
He is concerned and so ordains every moment and everyday of one's life,
He is conscious of every sparrow's fall and all of mankind's needs,
He is accurate as He neither sleeps nor slumbers, nor forgets His promises.

My unlimited God is everlasting, ever-present and always ready,
He is known in every part of the world and through history,
He is unlimited in His presence and power,
He is constant in this changing, unstable, unpredictable world of ours.

## INSPIRATIONS FOR THE MAN OF VALOUR

My unlimited God cannot be restricted by unbelief, doubt or fear,
He is unlimited in any situation in which man may find himself,
He is unlimited in the love bestowed on each lost one,
He is unlimited in His ability to bring the best out of the worst and weak.

My unlimited God can never be faulted by any known science or technology,
He cannot be accused of injustice, corruption, deceit, or unfaithfulness,
He cannot be overruled by any judge, king, force, power, or atomic bomb,
He cannot be questioned or asked to render an account or explanation.

My unlimited God can never be deceived by anyone at anytime,
For He sees right into every human heart, thought and intent,
He knows the end of all before the beginning, How great He is!
He hears every unsaid, whispered or shouted discussion and prayer.

He answers prayers properly directed to Him in faith,
He answers some whilst we are still thinking about phrasing them,
He answers others long after we have prayed and sometimes forgotten,
My unlimited God is a faithful, unfailing, caring and prayer-answering God!

Friend, is your god limited - in any place and at any time?
Is your god asleep, travelling, uncaring and unhelpful like Baal?
Is your god too weak and unable to defend himself like the smashed Baal?
Why not try my unlimited God, the unique and everlasting Trinity?[32]

---

[32] Luke 18:27; Mark 10:27; Isaiah 40:28: Jeremiah 32:27, Luke I : 28 – 37.

# GOD'S GREATNESS

The greatness of God is constantly revealed and in volumes,
In the vastness of the universe and the shape the same,
In the thickness of the forests and its numerous inhabitants,
The variety and nature of which is unique and yet complex.

The several miles stretch of seas around the world,
The depth of the same and several million litres of water they hold,
The variety of creatures within the sea each in its own right,
The individual characteristic of the seas and great oceans.

The clouds in the sky speak volumes as they move around,
Sometimes heavily loaded with water yet not complaining,
They carry this for many miles finally shedding it off as rain,
At other times they are light and white just like the cotton wool.

Watching the clouds could be very interesting and challenging,
Sometimes definite patterns and shapes made by the clouds can be seen,
Slow but steady they move in the sky without any failure,
To man, an approaching thick clouds signifies impending rain.

The delicate beautiful butterflies and moth display God's artistic nature,
And so are the beautiful plants and flowers especially in spring season,
The designs and colour combination of which inspires great artists,
And the skins of snakes and animals at home and in the forest.

## INSPIRATIONS FOR THE MAN OF VALOUR

The mysteries of God's creation, science cannot unravel completely,
The more man knows of any of God's creation the more remain unknown,
How great is our God who knew all of these before they were ever created,
He alone is the source of all wisdom, knowledge and faultless creativity.

O Lord my God, help me to appreciate Your greatness in my daily walk,
Doing my tasks, may I Your greatness reveal, Your love to my fellow man,
So that together we all might sing Your praises to You loving Father,
For Your greatness which is revealed in all creation and in several volumes.[34]

---

[34] John 1:3; Psalm 48:1; 95:3

INSPIRATIONS FOR THE MAN OF VALOUR

# PREPARE TO RECEIVE FROM GOD

We had been in this ship for months,
First we had forty days rain,
Then our ship tossed for the next one hundred and fifty days,
We went round the world believing in the One who locked us in.

On a particular day a bird was sent out,
For there was no weather forecast in those days,
It roamed around but came back in the evening,
Unable to find a place to land or rest.

A week later another bird was sent out,
It also went the whole day and; Guess what?
It brought back a fresh green olive plant in its mouth,
Our joy and happiness knew no bounds that evening.

Many days later patiently waiting in our ship,
Another bird was sent out like the others before,
Alas it did not return in the evening as expected,
Whao! It was now time for all to disembark our ship.

The bird is like the word of God to the people,
To the unbeliever, to save his soul from hell,
To the believer, to help in his earthly walk with God,
Unfortunately it may return if the condition is not right.

## INSPIRATIONS FOR THE MAN OF VALOUR

A believing heart is a prerequisite for receiving the word,
A grateful heart is a good soil when it finds one,
A believing heart in God is the first ingredient needed,
An obeying heart is the fruitful and rejoicing soil that yields multiples.

God's word is being sent daily to the world to benefit from,
But many have not believed nor positioned themselves to receive,
The words like the bird is on a specific mission and to bless you,
How good it will be for you to prepare to receive from God your Father?

Time to clean your heart, thought, mind and actions,
Time to believe His sent words are not meant to return to Him void,
Time to prepare the soil of your heart and life,
Time to joyfully expect a turnaround from the chaos to a peaceful life,
For the bird of your miracle has been sent out to locate you for your blessing.[35]

---

[35] James 1:21, Genesis 8:1-12

# 8

## *God's salvation plan*

*For God so loved the world, that he gave his only begotten Son,
that whosoever believeth in him should not perish,
but have everlasting life.
[John 3:16 (KJV)]*

*For God hath not appointed us to wrath,
but to obtain salvation by our Lord Jesus Christ,
Who died for us, that, whether we wake or sleep,
we should live together with him.
[1 Thessalonians 5:9-10 (KJV)]*

# DEATH

Death, death, death,
Very common yet least talked about,
Young people die and old people die,
Boys and girls die, men and women die too,
Africans, Asians, Caucasian, Jews all die,
Common to all people from all background,
Common to all tribes at all times of the day,
Common all week, month and all year round.

Some die from sickness, others die without sickness,
Some die from starvation, others die from overfeeding,
Some die from poverty, others die in their wealth,
Some die amidst their families, others without their families,
Some die in war or battle, others die amidst great peace,
Death ends it all for all people whenever it comes to them,
Nothing can stop anyone born of a woman from physical death.

Doctors and nurses, patients and others, good or bad die,
Kings, queens, princes, princesses and peasants die,
The wisest of the wise and the most stupid die too,
The best intellectuals and the non-intellectuals die,
The most successful and the unsuccessful in life die,
Single, married, separated or divorced people die too,
Death is a common denominator the Bible says.

There is physical death and there is spiritual death,
Physical death cuts you off from living here on earth,
Spiritual death cuts you off from living there in heaven,
Physical death cuts you off from your loved ones on earth,
Spiritual death cuts you off from your own Creator,
Physical death cannot be avoided by anyone,
Spiritual death can be avoided by all who choose to,
Only our Creator knows how each one will physically die.

Physical death is not the end of life as many people think,
Physical death is a result of our adamic sin,
Spiritual death is a result of unbelief in Jesus Christ,
Physical death is a passage to the continuation of life beyond,
Eternity of the soul of each person will be in heaven or hell,
For those who have Jesus Christ as their Lord in heaven,
For those who reject Jesus Christ as their Lord in hell,
Settle the continuation of your life beyond now,
Simply choose or reject Jesus.[36]

---

[36] Genesis 2:16-17; 3:1-19; John 3:16-18; Romans 3:23, 6:23.

INSPIRATIONS FOR THE MAN OF VALOUR

# HE FORGAVE ME

I should have been at the battlefield,
Fighting for my King and His people,
At home I got very bored,
Decided to take a walk on my balcony.

I saw the beautiful woman in the shower,
Couldn't take my eyes and mind off her,
I must have her I kept thinking,
Instructed my servants to get her for me.

I could not resist her beauty in her clothes,
Passionately and secretly I made love to her,
That she was another man's wife didn't matter,
Sent her home with some usual gifts I thought.

Weeks later my sins caught up with me,
My secret lover was carrying my seed I learnt,
A seed that couldn't be stopped from growing,
Soon it will be seen and the truth will be known.

I must find a way to cover up my mistake,
All attempts to deceive her husband failed,
He was much more a God-fearing man than I,
I had to organise his death with my army general.

## INSPIRATIONS FOR THE MAN OF VALOUR

He died as I had planned and hoped what a relief!
I had it all sorted out I breathed a sigh of relief,
Into my palace I brought my once secret lover,
Now to become my legitimate wife and lover.

He saw it all; I had forgotten but He sent me a word,
The prophet came with His judgement too hard to bear,
My son became very ill, I cried to Him,
Too late for he died because of my wicked acts.

I confessed my sins to Him for my lust and wickedness,
I repented of all the evil I had done to date known to me,
I made up my mind never to repeat that sin again,
He heard my confessions, cries and petitions at last.

He forgave me, He forgave me and He forgave me,
However at a costly price to myself, family now and later,
My secret sins were to be openly punished and rewarded,
He forgave me, He forgave me and He forgave me.

Friend, however bad or horrible your sins might be,
Even if you have killed or maimed before,
If you will acknowledge and confess your sins to Him,
He who forgave me will forgive you too.[37]

---

[37] 2 Samuel 11 – 12:19.

# BEHOLD THE WORLD SHAKER!

The world never heard a thing like this; a virgin conceived by the Holy Ghost.
A strange star shining in the East told the wise men a King was born,
And angels praising God on high, herald the glad tidings of joy,
To shepherds watching their flocks by night, all seated on the ground.

To King Herod the wise men went, to share with him the joyful news,
But Herod trembling in his loins, requests that word be brought to him that he
might go worship the king while feigning joy at the news from the wise men,
And when he saw he had been mocked, for the wise men did not return,
He ordered the killing of male children under two years old,
And the world also shook with fear

To the Jordan River He went, to be baptised of John,
The heavens opened and the Spirit of God like a dove; fell upon the Son of God,
The Father's voice rang loud and clear,
This is my beloved Son, in Him I am well pleased.

Here comes Satan in the wilderness, "… bow down and worship me"
But Jesus being full of the Spirit, answered him with the word,
Thou shall worship the Lord thy God and only Him shall you serve,
And angels came bowing to Him.

Enter His earthly ministry, the Scribes and Pharisees gaped with awe,
For He taught with great authority, not having been to school,
He healed all manner of diseases, demons took flight at His appearance,
Even the grave lost its power, dead men rose to live again.

## INSPIRATIONS FOR THE MAN OF VALOUR

At His death, the world stood still as unprecedented events took place,
The temple's curtain torn in two, gross darkness covered the earth at noon,
The earth quaked, hell's foundations shook and the tombs were open,
Dead men rose from the grave walked loose on planet earth.

On the third day, Life Himself arose from the grave, and the guard took flight,
The religious leaders shook with fear, "What manner of man is this?" they asked,
Through the city He went to show Himself till the city went agog with the news:
Christ is risen, we've seen the proof, death is destroyed and victory is won.

His duty done, and atonement made, up to heaven He ascended high,
The disciples and the crowd watched, as His body was lifted up,
An angel cried and told the crowd: men of Galilee, why do you stand …
Surely, this same Jesus will return, in the same way you've seen Him go.

Fifty days gone and here He comes, to keep His promise to the world,
Like the rushing of a mighty wind, the Comforter made His presence known,
Baptising all with cloven tongues of fire, till all men spoke another man's language

One more time and the world will behold Him face-to-face,
Just like they did when He arose,
With angels descending and saints ascending,
And every tongue confessing to His glory: He is Lord![38]

---

[38] Matthew 1: 18-25; 2; 3; 27:51-54; 28:1-12; Luke 24: 50-51; Acts 2:1-23

INSPIRATIONS FOR THE MAN OF VALOUR

# THE BEAUTY OF THE SNOW

Many children and adults like the time of snow every year,
Despite the cold, it is a time for many activities and excitements,
The snowball and snowman to make with families and friends,
Sledging in the park or on any available snow-covered land.

The power and the beauty of the snow cannot be imagined,
It is better personally experienced than being told by anyone,
The snow's uniqueness and beauty is worth waiting for,
And need not be a barrier to the normal day-to-day activities.

The snow falls in tiny flakes evenly across available open lands,
Covering every house or shed roofs, open land and cars outside,
In a matter of time everything uncovered outside gets covered,
Houses, sheds, trees, cars, buses, roads all become white.

The snow's pure whiteness adds a distinctive colour and beauty,
To every street, every road, every house and everything outside,
It has the ability of covering everything evenly however small or big,
Nothing can stand in its way once the snow starts to fall.

The dirt on every road is well covered with no protruding part,
Irrespective of previous painting, all houses becomes white,
Such is God's love capable of covering every sin from any man,
That it becomes undetectable to the sinner once he is forgiven.

God's love is available to all mankind irrespective of their background,
It is evenly spread and constant in its ability and availability,
As we expose our sins and weaknesses to His loving grace and mercy,
He turns us spotless and faultless, unique and beautiful unto Himself.

'Though your sins be as scarlet' God's promise to mankind says,
'Yet will I make them white as snow' the scripture tells us,
'Though they be red as crimson'
'Yet will I make them white as wool'.

The period of snow for many is a matter of a season,
Lasting between days and years in the arctic parts of the world
The beauty and the uniqueness can only be enjoyed so long as it lasts,
For then another season will soon be here according to God's plans.

The free gift of salvation dear friend is available now and free for all,
For many the opportunity comes once, for others many times,
This is the day and time of salvation friend, if you care to know,
For death comes once and after that comes God's judgement, not mercy.

Will you today accept the gift of salvation with its added benefits?
Experience the covering of your sins and past no matter how terrible,
Enjoy the cooling fall and anointing power of the blessed Holy Spirit,
Which today is falling everywhere, just like the beautiful snowflakes.[39]

---

[39] Psalm 147:16; Isaiah 1:18

# 9

## Facing the challenges of life

---

*That the trial of your faith,*
*being much more precious than of gold that perisheth,*
*though it be tried with fire,*
*might be found unto praise and honour and glory*
*at the appearing of Jesus Christ:*
*[1 Peter 1:7 (KJV)]*

*For his anger endureth but a moment;*
*in his favour is life:*
*weeping may endure for a night,*
*but joy cometh in the morning*
*[Psalms 30:5 (KJV)]*

# FACING THE PROBLEM

There are many methods of getting rid of problems, which come our way,
However, it is important that first, we recognise what the problem is,
Prayerfully searching the scriptures, we shall know how best to overcome it.

At the Red Sea, God instructed Moses to stretch forth the anointed rod,
That created a dry land in the sea for the children of Israel to pass through,
The same rod made the sea to return, destroying Pharaoh and his hosts.

The Jericho wall posed an obstacle to entering the Promised Land,
Had to be marched round once for six days and seven times on the seventh day,
With a loud shout unto the Lord, it all came crumbling down.

At war with the Israelites, the arrogant, experienced, boastful Goliath,
Was confronted by young, inexperienced but godly David in the Name of the Lord,
With five stones and a sling, Goliath fell and was beheaded with his own sword.

At the mercy of the creditors, the poor widow of the prophet and her two sons,
Sought God's counsel from Elisha the prophet,
Obedience to the prophet's instructions provided the needed money and more.

The prodigal son after coming back to his senses, realised his mistake,
Retraced his steps back home to his father in repentance and humility,
He was completely forgiven, restored and reinstated into the family.

## INSPIRATIONS FOR THE MAN OF VALOUR

The stormy sea, which had threatened to capsize the disciples' boat,
Made them wake up Master Jesus who was asleep in the boat,
He rebuked the wind, calmed the storm and peace was restored to the sea.

Attacked by a large army in evil confederacy, Jehoshaphat and the people,
Took their places and stood quietly watching God's miraculous deliverance,
As they sang aloud, songs of praises to the Lord who is mighty in battle.

As you face the problem beloved, recognising what it is all about,
You might have to confess, repent and retrace your steps back to God,
You might have to apply the word of God, which is the sword of the Spirit.

You might have to march round it in quietness and obedience to God,
You might have to attack it boldly like David in the name of the Lord.
You might have to seek for counsel from God's anointed ministers.

You might have to rebuke all the forces of attack in Jesus' Name,
You might have to joyfully praise the Lord and watch the enemies' defeat,
Beloved, with God on your side, you can face and defeat that problem.[40]

---

[40] 2Chro.20: 1-23, 1Sam 17: 1-54, Josh 6: 1-25, Exo.14: 1-31, 2Kgs 4: 1-7, Mark 4:35-41, Luke 15: 11-24

# NOT AN EASY ROAD

We all are pilgrims in this world,
Travelling towards eternity on a road,
Full of good times and bad times,
Enjoyment, hardships and temptations,
Aspirations, challenges and achievements,
Crossroads of daily decision taking.

It has no known human formula to use,
For each have diverse problems to face,
Whilst travelling on this road to eternity,
Mountains will be climbed along the way,
Valleys and rivers will be crossed too,
Daytime and dark times await each.

Travelling begins as soon as one is born,
No matter the race, tribe, sex or religion,
No matter the place one finds one self,
No matter what handicaps one has,
No matter what calling one has in life,
For all have been created by the same God.

Though not an easy road you may say,
With no known human formula to use or apply,
Walking with God would definitely make it easier,
If you will today ask Him into your heart and life,
He is ready to hold your hand and walk along,
With you on this road to eternity.[41]

[41] Matthew 7:14

# BLESSED BE THE NAME OF THE LORD

"Blessed be the name of the Lord"
What a difficult prayer for a child of God in trying times:
When a loved one dies, or his finances are torn apart,
When after all the effort, he fails an all-too-important examination,
When his body is ravaged with a cureless disease,
When it appears in spite of all his prayers,
God is very far away.

Whatever your challenging situation,
Pause and give Him thanks for praise is still comely unto Him
And blessed be the name of the Lord still,
Whether your day is filled with clouds or the sun comes shining through,
In everything just give Him thanks, the Bible commands you so,
His plans for you are all for good,
To give you a future and a hope.

Summers come and winters go,
Spring or autumn, all speak of change
But God is the same the seasons through
So is His mind concerning you, unchanging through thick and thin,
Family or friend, no one can turn Him from His purpose,
He sees your every tear; He hears your every sigh,
He's ever near, so don't give up your faith.[42]

---

[42] Job 1:21, 23:10 &13

INSPIRATIONS FOR THE MAN OF VALOUR

# THE TIDES

We live in a world which like the ocean surface is ripple full,
What with the very strong tides blowing periodically?
On each one no matter the race, colour, sex, age or size,
Sometimes very frightening are these tides, even to the child of God.

The tide may be strong enough to capsize the boat of anyone,
Leading to an unpredictable, expensive destruction and loss,
Especially for a non-believer who is like the house built on the sand,
This is different for a believer with strong anchor in the Lord.

For a child of God when the strong winds come,
Rather than capsizing our lifeboat and faith in God,
We are lifted higher and closer to God, the stronger the tide,
What more? We become better, believing and practising Christians.

The strong tide of jealousy made Joseph's brothers sell him,
To the Midian merchants who resold him to Portiphar in Egypt,
The strong tide of false accusation led to his indefinite imprisonment,
Which in the end led to his becoming Egypt's Governor.

The yearly tide of taunting by Peninnah,
Led the desperate barren Hannah to the tabernacle alone,
Crying out her heart out in silent words to the Almighty God,
God gave her Samuel the prophet and five other children.

# INSPIRATIONS FOR THE MAN OF VALOUR

The incoming strong tide of death from Pharaoh the King,
Led to Moses' running to the land of Midian for forty years,
There he got a wife, had two children and what's more?
He received God's personal commission to lead Israel out of Egypt.

The unquenchable tide of jealousy and impending death,
Made David to abandon his post at the palace of Saul,
Running and roaming in the wilderness for many years,
Which became his preparation as a king, poet and music composer.

The callous and unsympathetic tide of the loan collector,
Drove the widow to Prophet Elisha for help and counsel,
Not only did she experience the miracle of the flowing olive oil,
She paid off her debt and had the security of her children.

The strong tide of ignorance and foolishness of the devil,
Made the Pharisees to crucify Jesus Christ on the cross,
What was supposed to end His life, brought eternal life,
To mankind of every generation and race who will believe in Him.

The strong tide of wickedness of the Jews of that time,
Led to the many sufferings of Paul especially that of imprisonment,
What a blessing in disguise as Paul's letters in the Bible were written,
While serving his prison sentence in chains in the jail.

Today you too might be facing a strong tide,
Which might seem overwhelming and life threatening,
Cheer up for underneath the strong tide of trials and tribulations,
Lies the Sovereign God's triumph and unimaginable blessings.[43]

[43] Psalm 107:29

INSPIRATIONS FOR THE MAN OF VALOUR

# 10

## *Wisdom for living*

---

*Wisdom is the principal thing; therefore get wisdom: and with all thy getting get understanding.*
*[Proverbs 4:7 (KJV)]*

*For wisdom is better than rubies; and all the things that may be desired are not to be compared to it.*
*[Proverbs 8:11 (KJV)]*

# NO CARELESS WORD

Many words are spoken today,
At different places, to different people,
By different authorities of different powers.

While some words are carelessly spoken,
Others are spoken without giving it a thought,
Others are spoken with no intention of fulfilment.

Some words are carefully chosen by the authorities,
With every thought and weight to every communication,
Realising how important words could be to each party.

Many leaders of old and of today,
Have made unrealistic, unreasonable promises,
Knowing quite well that such cannot be kept.

Other leaders or parents at other times and places,
Have made promises believing they could fulfil them,
Alas! They are unable, as the circumstances get beyond their control.

Some parents have spoken to their children,
Promising them what they can never afford to give,
And dashing the children's hopes.

God's words are never carelessly spoken,
Whether directly to the individual, group or nation,
Whether through the written word or prophetic messages.

His words will certainly come to pass,
Irrespective of the time, place and people concerned,
Irrespective of the prevailing negative circumstances around.

No careless word from the Almighty God,
He means every word written or prophetically spoken,
He watches over His words to bring them to pass.

No careless word from the Almighty, all knowing God,
Whether they are words of healing, blessing or anointing,
Or they are words of punishment or justice.

Over and over again God confirms His words,
In the lives of His people no matter their level of faith,
At His own appointed time and chosen manner.

What has God spoken to you now or before
That seems impossible, unfulfilled or completely forgotten?
It will certainly come to pass, as God speaks no careless word.[44]

---

[44] Isaiah 55: 10 -11, Psalms 12:6.

# THE APPOINTED TIME OF THE LORD

In God's own plan for us,
There is a time for everything,
A time for each child of His,
To receive His promises to them.

For Abraham and Sarah,
The promise of a child to them,
Was fulfilled some twenty five years,
After they first heard the promise from Him.

For Joseph the son of Jacob,
The promise of being a leader,
Came about thirteen years later,
After being a slave and prisoner.

The promise of deliverance,
For the Israelites in Egypt,
Was manifest over 400 years later,
When Moses and Aaron were commissioned.

The promise of salvation at Eden,
Became fulfilled at Christ's birth,
God had to come in human form,
To reconcile us back to Himself.

In God's time are all things,
Made beautifully and perfectly,
Though the vision tarries,
It shall certainly come to pass.

What has the Lord promised you?
Though it seems delayed now,
Believing Him, relax completely,
A thousand years is like a day to Him.

Wait my brother, tarry my sister,
For God's own appointed time for you,
For God's timing is always accurate,
Never too early or late in His actions.[45]

---

[45] Habakkuk 2:3.

INSPIRATIONS FOR THE MAN OF VALOUR

# TOUCH SOMEONE TODAY

There are five senses in a human being,
The sense of sight, hearing and smelling,
That of tasting and touching,
Through which messages are received and relayed.

However, the power of touch is so real,
While others could be easily mistaken or unnoticed.
That of touch cannot be mistaken or easily forgotten,
Especially in times of great needs of man.

No wonder the Rabbi begged Jesus for a touch,
On His little daughter who had just died at home.
Great was his faith in Jesus' healing power,
That would raise the dead girl just by a mere touch.

The unnamed woman with the issue of blood,
Had suffered for twelve years in the hands of all.
Despised, rejected, weak, feeble, faint and weary,
She sought for complete healing from Jesus Christ.

Aware of the difficulties to be encountered,
She was content with touching Jesus' garment.
For she believed that would procure the desired healing,
What joy as her faith was honoured and recognised!

## INSPIRATIONS FOR THE MAN OF VALOUR

'Stir up the gift of God' Paul admonished Timothy,
Which was given to you when hands were laid upon your head,
Being no longer afraid of anything,
But filled with power, love and a strong mind.

Stop underestimating the touch of the Almighty God,
Released on you through God's messengers, dear friend,
Begin today to flow in God's mighty power,
Unto every being you come in contact with.

Be kind to give a friendly touch dear brother,
To that person you know needs your help now,
To that very sick child and the worried parent,
Let them feel God's love and power through your touch.

God is able to bring about the miracle through you,
Identify with that person's problem today,
As you reach out to touch him and the need,
If anything, dear friend, touch someone today.[46]

---

[46] Acts 10:38

# 11

## The awesome and Omnipotent God

# NAME

Everything in this world has a name,
By which it is called and identified,
But have you stopped to ponder why,
Each article, place or person is named?

What is in a name you may ask?
If not to identify and differentiate,
Much is in a name you may wish to know,
Such that God gave names after each creation.

There is none of God's creature without a name,
However minute, small big in size or shape,
There is no problem or disease without a name,
There is no feeling or achievement without a name.

There is nothing under heaven without a name,
Whilst some names bring along joy and hope,
Some names connote failure and depression,
Some other names bring along doubt and fear.

However there is a name above all the names,
Both in heaven and under the earth,
To which every knee must bow at its mention,
Every tongue confess, yea the name of Jesus Christ!

What is the name of that thing, friend?
That has brought your heartache for so long?
That has caused fear to run down your spine?
That has made you restless and sleepless?

Why will you continue to suffer dear friend?
When the solution to your problem is here?
Why not call on that name of Jesus Christ?
And experience victory over those other names?[47]

---

[47] Philippians 2:9; Psalm 148:13

# GOD TO THE PROFESSIONALS

To the Astrologer, God is the Bright and Morning Star,
To the Baker, God is the Bread of life,
To the Banker, God is the unfailing Provider,
To the Builder, God is the Chief Cornerstone,

To the Carpenter, God is the Door to eternal life,
To the Cook, God is the Salt of the world,
To the Doctor, God is the Great Physician,
To the Electrician, God is the Light of the world,

To the Farmer, God is the Sower,
To the Florist, God is the Rose of Sharon, the Lily of the valley,
To the Geologist, God is the Rock of Ages,
To the Geriatrist, God is the Ancient of Days,

To the Geographer, God is the Way of life,
To the Instructor, God is the Divine Instructor,
To the Judge, God is the soon-coming Judge of the world,
To the King, God is the King of Kings and soon-coming King,

To the Lawyer, God is the Defender of the poor,
To the Lord, God is the Lord of lords,
To the Military, God is the Mighty warrior, Deliverer and Commander In Chief,
To the Nomads and animal rearers, God is the Great Shepherd,

## INSPIRATIONS FOR THE MAN OF VALOUR

To the Nurse, God is the unforgetful Nursing Mother,
To the Pastor, God is the Keeper of the flock,
To the Priest, God is the High Priest,
To the Radiographer, God is the X-Ray that sees into every human heart,

To the transporter, God is the Way of life,
To the Senator, God is the lawgiver,
To the Soldier, God is the Man of war,
To the Teacher, God is the Good Teacher.

To the Ultrasonographer, God is the sound that sees our unformed bodies.
To the husbandman, God is the Vinedresser.
To the surveyor, God is the way maker
Who is God to you?[48]

---

[48] Colossians 1:17

## JUST A TOUCH

For twelve years she suffered,
In the hands of many doctors,
And none could help her,
Until she met with Jesus,
It was just a touch of Jesus' garment,
And she became perfectly healed.

For several years he suffered,
In the hands of leprosy,
The society abandoned Him,
Until he met with Jesus,
It was just a touch from Jesus,
That cleansed his leprosy.

Twelve year old Jairus' daughter,
Laid very sick in bed,
Her father went to seek Jesus,
Before He came she was dead,
But just a touch and word from Jesus,
Brought her back to life.

What then is your illness?
Doctors have not helped you much,
Friend, there is a way out,
Accept Jesus as your Lord,
And just a touch from Jesus,
Will meet that need of yours.[49]

[49] Mark 5:22-42

# THE SAME GOOD LORD MADE THEM ALL

Some are tall and some are short,
Some are thin and some are fat,
Some are rich and some are poor,
Some are young and some are old.

Some have plenty of hair and some are bald,
Some have good health and some are sick,
Some are wise and some are foolish,
Some are learned and some are not.

Some are brown and some are pink,
Some are dark and some are light,
Some are males and some are females,
The good Lord, made them all.

# DO YOU LOVE YOURSELF?

Love your neighbour as yourself
Is the Biblical injunction to all
But the question comes to mind
Do you love yourself dear friend?

Many want to love their neighbours
As themselves many a times
Yet they do not love themselves
Enough to transfer this love to others.

You have been hearing the salvation message
Over and over again from many people
Do you love yourself enough to accept
Jesus Christ as your Lord and Saviour?

Do you love yourself as a child in the home
Respecting your parents and those older than you?
Do you fulfil all your family obligations?
To merit a long life full of blessing?.

Do you love yourself as a student
In your attendance at lectures?
Is your submission of assignments timely?
How hard do you study for examinations?

Do you love yourself in your marital relationship?
Is your marriage based on God's principles?
Is it based on monogamy and permanency?
Is it based on fidelity and love?

God has blessed you with riches and talents
Do you love yourself enough to give them back to Him
As you give willingly to the spread of the gospel?
And wisely utilise your talents to bless mankind?

Do you love yourself in your self evaluations?
Are your confessions negative or positive?
Is your thought true, pure, lovely, good and right?
How much do you pray for yourself?

Self is one's greatest enemy
The flesh lusts against the spirit
What you want to do that you don't do
What you don't want is what you do.

'Charity begins at home' is the saying of the wise
Start to love yourself from now
In your thoughts, utterances and actions
Then loving your neighbour will be easy for you.

---

[49] Mark 5:22-42 , Philippians 4:8, Matthew 19:19 & Romans 8:21-25

# INSPIRATIONS FOR THE MAN OF VALOUR

*Dear Reader,*

*Thank you for your time and resources committed to supporting this writing ministry. Please help to tell others about how much the Lord has blessed you reading this book.*

*You will certainly be blessed by the other books written by Oluwakemi, so why not visit www.protokospublishers.com and place an order today.*

*It will equally be appreciated if you can help to write a few sentences review of the book on www.amazon.com and/or on www.protokospublishers.com*

*Please note that all our books are easily available on our website and in other good bookshops.*

*God bless you as you do.*
*Management*
*Protokos Publishers.*

## OPPORTUNITY TO BECOME A CHRISTIAN

*Dear Father in heaven,*
*Thank you for the privilege of reading this book. Indeed I have sinned and come short of Your glory. I am grateful to You for sending Jesus Christ into this world to come to die on the cross of Calvary for me. I believe in my heart that Jesus Christ paid for my sins, past, present and future. I believe Jesus Christ was buried and on the third day He rose from the dead. I believe that Jesus Christ will come back again. I confess with my mouth and I accept Him now to be my Lord.*

*Master, Saviour, Brother, and Friend, I ask in Your mercy for the infilling of the Holy Spirit so that with His help, I can live a victorious life becoming all that You have ordained me to be in Jesus' name. I pray with thanksgiving. Amen.*

## CONGRATULATIONS YOU ARE BORN AGAIN!

*If after reading this book you said the above prayer and became born-again, Congratulations! You are Born Again is a booklet for those who have done so through reading this book. It is a free booklet that we would like you to have. In it, the frequently asked questions are answered and this will get you on the way to growing in your newfound faith in God. You can download this free booklet from our website:* ***www.protokospublishers.com***

*You may also contact any of the organisations listed at the end of the book.*

*I look forward to hearing from you soon.*
*O. Ola –Ojo (2015)*

## Other Books By The Author:

### Provocation, Prayer and Praise
(December 2004 & 2009)

Complimentary to The Christian and Infertility this book focuses on the story of an infertile woman in the Bible, her provocations, prayer and praise. Whatever makes you incomplete, unfulfilled, less than whom God made you to be, whatever issue of life that the enemy uses to provoke you calls for prayer.

**Key features include:**
- Some known medical reasons for infertility in the women.
- Why Hannah went to the house of God in spite of her barrenness.
- Is it true that the husband is much more than 10 sons to the infertile woman?
- When, where and how to address the source/cause of your provocation.
- God is able to meet that humanly impossible need of yours.
- God's part and your part in that promise.
- Time to celebrate and praise God.

**Book Details:**
Paperback: 128 pages
Language English
ISBN-13: 978-0-9557898-3-0

**Review:**
An excellent easy to read and understand book. The principles shared in this book though primarily are for those trying for a baby could as well be applied to any area of hurt and un-fulfillment.

Reviewer: A Reader from London, 7 Jan 2006 on Amazon.co.uk

 :www.protokospublishers.co.uk

# INSPIRATIONS FOR THE MAN OF VALOUR

## The Christian and Infertility
(December 2004 & 2009)

The Christian and Infertility addresses one of the often neglected needs of Christian couples. It gives an insight into infertility from the biblical and medical perspectives. It is written not only for potential fruitful couples but for pastors, family and friends of these couples. It is written that the Body of Christ might be fully equipped to know and support couples who are facing the challenge of infertility at present

**Key features include:**
- Childlessness in the Bible and lessons to learn;
- Some known spiritual causes of infertility;
- The man and low sperm count;
- Some possible physical, medical and environmental causes of infertility;
- Some of the available treatment options in the UK;
- Choice of fertility treatment;
- Should a Christian professional be involved in fertility treatment?

**Book Details:**
Paperback: 146 pages
Language English
ISBN-13: 978-0-9557898-2-3

**Review:**
The book is a great eye-opener for all. It sheds light on infertility from the medical and spiritual angle. This gives the reader a balance because i believe every human being is made up of both physical and spiritual part. To get a balance in life, the two parts must be well fed. One must not concentrate on the spiritual and neglect the physical part. The book also reminds us that God has a way of sorting us out. The book is quite inspiring. I will recommend this book to everybody trusting God for any form of blessing from God to go get one and apply it to his or her situation. It will definitely bless you and yours'.

Reviewer: A reader from Glen Burnie, USA, 29 Oct 2007 on Amazon.co.uk

:www.protokospublishers.co.uk

INSPIRATIONS FOR THE MAN OF VALOUR

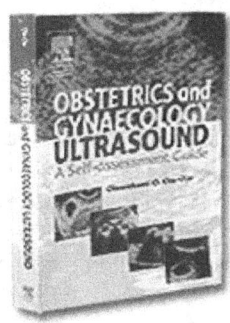

## Obstetrics and Gynaecology Ultrasound -
A Self-Assessment Guide
June 2005 Churchill Elsevier Publishers, UK.

This self-assessment guide is a structured questions and answer book that develops the reader's understanding capability using a simple method in treating related topics. Clinical indications are presented with their corresponding ultrasound findings using appropriate illustrations. A case study approach is followed; presenting the clinical and ethical dilemmas that might arise whilst encouraging students to think.
The aim is to reinforce theoretical knowledge within a clinical environment.

**Key features:**
- Includes a detailed study of fertility.
- Aids quick understanding of subject matter.
- Over 600 high-resolution ultrasound images.
- Cover a wide spectrum of ultrasound curriculum.

**Book Details:**
- Paperback: 468 pages
- ISBN-10: 0443064628
- ISBN-13: 978-0443064623

**Review:**
"...This excellent new book is a study guide... This is an attractive paperback that should be essential reading for trainee obstetric and gynaecological sonographers, whether they are radiographers or radiology or obstetric trainees. It will be of particular value to those preparing for the RCOG/RCR Diploma in Advanced Obstetric Ultrasound and to specialist registrars in obstetrics and gynaecology undertaking special skills modules in fetal medicine, gynaecological ultrasound and infertility..."

The Obstetrician & Gynaecologist, www.rcog.org.uk/togonline
Book reviews 2006

Reviewer : Ann Harper MD FRCPI FRCOG.
Consultant Obstetrician and Gynaecologist
Royal Jubilee Maternity Service, Belfast., UK

 :www.protokospublishers.co.uk

INSPIRATIONS FOR THE MAN OF VALOUR

## GOOD MUMS, BAD MUMS
*(June 2005 & 2009)*

This is in two parts, the main chapter that can be used for personal or group study, and an accompanying exercise section. The privileged position of a mother is in her being a co-creator with God and bringing forth life (lives). This book compliments one of God's previous revelations to me as contained in the book titled Good Dads, Bad Dads'. While the father could be likened to the pilot of the family plane, the mother can be likened to the force behind the plane – positive or negative. Good mothers are not only co-creators with God, they also do nurture as well as nourish their children physically, emotionally and spiritually.

**Keys Features:**
- Were all the mothers in the Bible good mothers?
- Be motivated in the areas of your strengths.
- Learn ways of supporting your husband and children.
- Lessons from the strengths and weakness of 7 mothers.
- Be encouraged - you are not alone in the assignment of motherhood.

**Book Details:**
- Paperback: 162 pages
- Language : English
- ISBN-13: 978-0-9557898-1-6

**Review:**
I appreciate the author's method of writing. It is always exciting holding her book to read. Personally, 'Good Mums, Bad Mums' has been a blessing to me in no small measure. The book is rich, it is loaded with physical and spiritual uplifting subjects. To all existing and potential mothers, this book is a MUST read. At the end of every chapter there is an exercise to do that will help in re-examining your life spiritually and in other ways. I encourage all women to get and use this book as a guide in raising their children. You will be glad you did.

Reviewer: Pastor Mrs T Adegoke
Freedom Arena
London, UK

 :www.protokospublishers.co.uk

## To the Bride with Love
*(2007 & 2009)*

Every wise woman preparing to get married knows she will need sound advice, practical tips and solid, heartfelt prayers, of those who have travelled on the road she is about to journey on. In this book, 10 women of different age groups, from different backgrounds and cultures who wedded under various circumstances, individually share their experience with the bride in an intimate, very candid and unforgettable way

**Keys Features:**
- Learn from 10 married women.
- Find your divine purpose in marriage.
- Learn what and how to feed your family.
- Be blessed by prayers from your guests.
- Receive remarkable gifts for your marriage.

**Book details:**
Paperback: 108 pages
Language: English
ISBN-13: 978-0-9557898-4-7

To the Bride with Love is the perfect bride's evergreen companion. The content is suitable, relevant and applicable even decades after the wedding day.

To the Bride with Love is an ideal wedding gift on its own. It can also accompany any other gift (big or small) that you have for the bride but take this hint... the bride will keep thanking you for the book years and years after.

**Reviews:**
'One of the best', This book has really helped my marriage from the onset as I got it as a wedding gift, God bless the giver. It's a must read for relationship improvement and God's guidance. I recommend it for people to get it for themselves, moreover as a great blessing for someone else in love. "To the Bride with Love"
Reviewer: **Sade Olaoye** "clare4good" (United Kingdom) 19 Jul 2008 on Amazon.com

**Another Review:**

The writing style of Oluwakemi is unique, peculiar and distinct to herself. I recommend To the Bride with Love to wives, wives to be, mothers, mentors, youth leaders and workers. Why? The clarity, the focus and the intent of this book is so empowering, encouraging and enlightening that it will definitely mold or re mold a life to achieve its purpose. The truth is, there are very few books that have depth as well as help you to achieve your goals and arrive at your destination. Many books tend to excite you but have no depth; you read and you forget; they do not really change you but this book, To the Bride with Love will definitely leave a word in your spirit and move you to your next level!

I believe that this is also a book that pastors will find useful as a manual for marriage counseling, because many books on marriage focus mostly on what you as an individual can gain, your own personal satisfaction while little is said about the sacrifices involved and their importance. As my pastor usually says, it is important to learn from those who have gone ahead, understand why some were successful and others weren't, so that we won't fall where they fell, rather, we would gain more speed, achieve our goals and thereby glorify Christ.

So, I invite you not only to get a copy of this life-changing manual for yourself, but also to put it into as many hands as you can afford to, for then the world will definitely benefit and your life will be a blessing to many.

Reviewer: Oyinlola Odunlami CEO.
Shallom Bookshop, London UK

 :www.protokospublishers.co.uk

INSPIRATIONS FOR THE MAN OF VALOUR

## Refuge Under His Wings

"an exhaustive analysis of the Book of Ruth in the Bible. The author combines her deep Christian conviction and excellent knowledge of the Holy Scriptures to produce a must read for every Christian, married or single. The book is interspaced with beautifully written prayers, which enables the reader to pause, pray and meditate on the revelations received... The book is also loaded with poetry like 'Thy will be done oh Lord' for those who may be facing an uncertain future or on a cross road of decisions."

**Key Features:**
- Famine in the land whose fault?
- Do I relocate in famine times and where to?
- Back to God, back to blessings.
- Finding refuge Under His Wings.
- A new beginning and a new song

**Book details:**
Paperback: 100 pages
Language: English
ISBN-10: 095578980X
ISBN-13: 978-0955789809

**Review:**
This book feeds the soul. Most of all I loved the poetry. It gives you time to savour the thoughts as reader. There is a good mix of poetry and prose. To look at the story of Ruth in depth gave good spiritual food. You can pause and take it in at your own pace.The meditation on Psalm 121 was good also. There's nothing like reading a Psalm slowly and meditating on its contents. The author's own reflections allow you to see the book through someone else's eyes. A good read.

Reviewer : Gaby Richards,
London, UK.

 :www.protokospublishers.co.uk

# INSPIRATIONS FOR THE MAN OF VALOUR

## GRACE OR WORKS?

This book makes you examine a lot of issues in your life, family relationships in particular, that you may have taken for granted or totally ignored. As conveyed right from the rhetorical question posed in the title, Grace or Works, the author stirs you towards asking yourself pertinent questions, thinking through for answers and even getting solutions for unresolved problems.

Have you heard of prodigal wives, husbands, mothers or prodigal fathers? This book identifies and defines them clearly. For anyone experiencing a crises in their relationship with such prodigal family members, this book, which is based on the parable of the "Prodigal son" in Luke 15:11-32 is a one-stop resource material to meet your counseling needs. And just in case you happen to be the prodigal who has caused your relatives much sorrow, there is hope for you in this book.

Interspersed with prayers for you by the author and specific prayers that you can say for yourself, as well as poems to comfort and inspire you, Grace or Works not only asks you questions, it helps you make and maintain the right choices.

**Key Features:**
- Right request but wrong timing.
- God's gifting and our free will.
- Abroad but for the wrong reasons.
- Time to return home
- A father's unmerited favour.
- 'Shut out' of celebrations because of anger.
- You did not have because you did not ask.

**Book details:**
Paperback: 122 pages
Language: English
ISBN-13: 978-0-9557898-5-4

 :www.protokospublishers.co.uk

# THERE IS A REWARD FOR PARENTING

Man may claim that the conception of a particular child was accidental, but in God's eyes every child is in His plan and has a purpose and mission to fulfill here on earth. As a parent, teacher, church or community leader, how are you treating the children in your care?

God does not sleep nor slumber; are you sure you are doing what He expects of you as a parent or children's Sunday school teacher? What kind of reward do you expect from Him?

There is a Reward for Parenting provides a lot of answers and food for thought, using scriptural principles to show you how to ensure a good reward from God in the unique assignment of parenting and child care.

As characteristic of Oluwakemi Ola-Ojo's previous books, there is a free gift of her poems at the end of this book also, to add value to the content of the main text – making it two books for the price of one!

**Key Features:**
- Every child counts.
- The making of a winner.
- You need wisdom.
- Good and bad parenting.

**Book details:**
Paperback: 88 pages
Language : English
ISBN 978-0-9557898-6-1

**Review:**
The book is lovely, inspiring, very educative both spiritually and secularly.

Reviewer : **M.F.Owoeye**. Lagos- Nigeria

 :www.protokospublishers.co.uk

INSPIRATIONS FOR THE MAN OF VALOUR

## Let's Reason Together ...Youths' A-Z (Book 1)

According to the United Nations demographic statistics, the global youth population, ranging in age from 15 to 24 years, today stands at more than 1.5 billion, representing about 22 percent or a fifth of the world's 6.8 billion people inhabiting the earth. In developing nations where a greater number of this group resides, the youth population sometimes gets as high as 60% or more of the total population of such nations!

Since it is also globally accepted that the youth of any nation forms the strength of that nation, economically, militarily and/or otherwise, it is imperative that this group of people cannot be overlooked.

It is against this backdrop that the book, **LET'S REASON TOGETHER – YOUTH'S A-Z** is a timely one that is set to address the various issues that affect young people as well as their vision and aspirations. Since the primary goal of young people is to live full lives in their societies, this book examines specific elements that would help them in this process. It covers a wide range of issues from the sublime such as attitude, choices, education, health and xenophobia to the seemingly mundane such as dreams, integrity and vacation.

### Key Features:
- A relevant word per alphabet.
- A time to reflect on the key word.
- An easy phrase per alphabet to remember.
- 3 prayer points per alphabet to help you pray.

### Book details:
- Paperback: 316 pages
- ISBN 978-0-9557898-7-8

### Review:
This is the most wonderful piece of youth work I have ever seen, capturing diverse situations and circumstances peculiar to youths. The work is thorough, educative and spiritually exhilarating. It is a must have for every youth worker to use, either in group discussions, seminars or straightforward teaching. This piece of work will yet raise the gospel abroad.

Reviewer: **Dr M Akindele**, Consultant Paediatrician, London, UK

 :www.protokospublishers.co.uk

# INSPIRATIONS FOR THE MAN OF VALOUR

## Let's Reason Together
## ...Youths' A-Z (Book 2)

According to the United Nations demographic statistics, the global youth population, ranging in age from 15 to 24 years, today stands at more than 1.5 billion, representing about 22 percent or a fifth of the world's 6.8 billion people inhabiting the earth. In developing nations where a greater number of this group resides, the youth population sometimes gets as high as 60% or more of the total population of such nations!

Since it is also globally accepted that the youth of any nation forms the strength of that nation, economically, militarily and/or otherwise, it is imperative that this group of people cannot be overlooked.

It is against this backdrop that the book, **LET'S REASON TOGETHER – YOUTH'S A-Z** is a timely one that is set to address the various issues that affect young people as well as their vision and aspirations. Since the primary goal of young people is to live full lives in their societies, this book examines specific elements that would help them in this process. It covers a wide range of issues from the sublime such as anger, drugs, examination, homosexuality, jealousy and rejection to the seemingly mundane such as growth, ignorance and youth etc.

### Key Features:
- A relevant word per alphabet.
- A time to reflect on the key word.
- An easy phrase per alphabet to remember.
- 3 prayer points per alphabet to help you pray.

### Book details:
Paperback: 322 pages
Language: English
ISBN : 978-0-9557898-9-2

### Review:
This is a must read for the youths and anyone that deals with teenagers. All Sunday school staff will benefit from this book.
Reviewer: **Deaconess B. Josiah**. London, UK

 :www.protokospublishers.co.uk

# GOOD DADS, BAD DADS

This is a timeless book for men of all generations. It is very pragmatic, informative and honest in its outlook and aims to be some resource of great support and guidance to fathers specifically and men in general.

It tackles such issues as showing favouritism, unconditional love, keeping pledges, providing for the family, building an altar of worship, obedience to God's voice and the importance of leadership in the home among others.

It is a very good indicator for men who want to ensure that peace, love and orderliness reign supreme in their homes and all other endeavours of life they are involved in. It is by no means exhaustive in its nature but acts as a pointer to the ageless truths found in the Bible. It challenges men to be all that they can be for the good of the society they live in and most of all the best fathers any children may ever desire to have. It is based on some Biblical characters, all of whom are very different one from the other with their flaws and areas of excellence in order that the good father today might eschew their short-comings and pursue those aspects of these biblical characters that are worthy.

To ensure that fathers continually transform their lives, there is an accompanying workbook to stimulate them and to keep the nuggets found in this book close to their hearts which in turn reflects in the way they live their lives.

Key Features:
- Written especially for today's father in mind.
- Be blessed as you read about 12 other fathers.
- Learn what makes a father good or bad.
- Explore the pains and gains of fatherhood.
- Learn from the secrets of successful fathers.
- Learn from the failures of unsuccessful fathers.
- Learn what your child/ren and wife want from you.

**Book details:**
Paperback: 230 pages
Language English
ISBN 978-1-908015-00-6

 :www.protokospublishers.co.uk

# INSPIRATIONS FOR THE MAN OF VALOUR

**Review:**

*"Just a note to say that the book 'Good Dads Bad Dads' is a powerful and thought-provoking book".*

Reviewer: **Prof A. I. Sodeye** - United Kingdom

**Review**
Primarily, I find the book pleasurable to read and understand. To the spiritually inclined, the book is prophetic and as you read along you get the impression that it is not just discussing a topic, but expressing and bringing to light, real life situations. The book is quite engaging and provides an avenue for readers to reflect and take stock as they read along.

As a pastor, I realise that most of the fatherhood problems were highlighted maturely but factually. The author provides the opportunity to receive fresh insights from what is practicable and on-going in human affairs - duties and responsibilities of fathers. Additionally, the book is appropriate in that, absentee-fathers who are privileged to read or hear from someone who has read the book, would have an opportunity to repent and reduce the number of such men to a negligible few.

Furthermore the book is filled with wisdom and encouragement for anyone doing well as a father and, for those who are not really there yet, the author offers hope, contact details and prayers of repentance. I salute the writer for effective communication on a sensitive topic such as this. The book, 'Good dads, Bad Dads' is not judgemental or sentimental, but it is timely, culturally relevant and once read, you will like to read it again. I recommend this book to all serious dads and to those hoping to be one!

Reviwer: **Pastor Isaac Ajibolorunrin**
Christ The Lord Tabernacle, London UK.

:www.protokospublishers.co.uk

# INSPIRATIONS FOR THE MAN OF VALOUR

## GOOD DADS, BAD DADS (Work Book)

This is a timeless book for men of all generations. It is very pragmatic, informative and honest in its outlook and aims to be some resource of great support and guidance to fathers specifically and men in general.

It tackles such issues as showing favouritism, unconditional love, keeping pledges, providing for the family, building an altar of worship, obedience to God's voice and the importance of leadership in the home among others.

It is a very good indication for men who want to ensure that peace, love and orderliness reign supreme in their homes and all other endeavours of life they are involved in. It is not at all exhaustive in its nature but acts as a pointer to the ageless truths found in the Bible. It challenges men to be all that they can be for the good of the society they live in and most of all the best fathers any child(ren) may ever desire to have.

To ensure that fathers continually transform lives, this is the accompanying workbook to stimulate them and to keep the nuggets found close to their hearts which in turn reflects in the way they live their lives.

**Key Features:**
Essentially for the present day father. This workbook allows you:
- To be encouraged and motivated as a father.
- To use it as an individual or in a men's group.
- Time to reflect on the lives of the 12 fathers you have read.
- Opportunity to identify your own strengths and weakness.
- To have relevant prayer points to help you pray in your role.

**Book details:**
Paperback : 152 pages
Language : English
ISBN : 978-1-908015-01-3

 :www.protokospublishers.co.uk

# INSPIRATIONS FOR THE MAN OF VALOUR

## ABC of PEOPLE and THINGS in the BIBLE

This Workbook 'ABC of People and Things in the Bible' is specifically written for the 6-8 year old as a corresponding tool to help the child learn and practice the lessons taught from the book, ABC of People and Things in the Bible. It provides a series of basic do-it-yourself activities such as reading, writing and drawing.

The workbook is a perfect teaching aid that enables the child to express him/herself and helps the parent/teacher to identify the depth of the child's understanding or otherwise of the lessons taught.

**Key Features:**
- Hours of learning and fun at the same time.
- Encourage child's self-confidence in reading.
- Encouraging good handwriting through practice.
- Unique and personalized workbook for your child.
- Easy way to monitor's child's developments and creativity
- Opportunity for your child's creativity to be developed/enhanced.

**Book details:**
Paperback: 64 pages
Language English
ISBN 978-1-908015-05-1

Review:
I love the entire concept - creatively teaching the Bible through Bible stories and creatively teaching how to write in a fun and in an Interactive way.

Reviewer: **O. Ukaejiofo.** UK.

 :www.protokospublishers.co.uk

# INSPIRATIONS FOR THE MAN OF VALOUR

## ABC of PEOPLE and THINGS in the BIBLE
### (Parent/Teachers Manual 1)

Creative! That is the only word to describe Oluwakemi Ola-Ojo's new book, ABC of People and Things in the Bible. Many Christian parents desire to give their children an early start in Christian living and discipline through the knowledge of the Bible but simply do not know how. The reason for this is not farfetched. Teaching a six-year old is not exactly a dinner date, or is it?

ABC of People and Things in the Bible provides the perfect answer to this challenge. The book presents a highly efficient way of teaching 6-8 year-olds the Bible in a friendly yet educative manner. Using the letters of the English alphabet, Oluwakemi Ola-Ojo details the lives of people in the Bible, to teach children moral values that will help to shape their lives as well as helping them to identify and avoid mistakes that destroyed the lives of some of the characters mentioned.

The book comes highly recommended as a teaching aid not just in Sunday school but in regular school classes as well as private home studies.

### Key Features:

Essentially for the present day Parent/Teacher. This manual allows you:
- To learn at the Creator's feet.
- To learn about many people in the Bible.
- To have wholesome discussions with your child
- To adapt the various teachings to the level of child.
- To teach your child line-upon line, precept –upon - precept
- Gives you many hours of learning and fun together with the child.

### Book details:

Paperback: 112 pages
Language: English
ISBN 978-1-908015-04-4

:www.protokospublishers.co.uk

INSPIRATIONS FOR THE MAN OF VALOUR

## ABC of Place and Things in the Bible - Child's Workbook (Age 9-10)

This is a work tool that comes as a complimentary companion to the book, ABC of Places and Things in the Bible. It is an interactive manual designed to assist the child's learning, by providing him/her the opportunity to read and to commit to memory, the contents of the book. The workbook also helps to improve the child's writing and drawing skills, and gives him/her room to explore and express his/her creative ability in any or all of these areas while having fun in the process.

There is no doubt that the workbook is a practical aid to learning for 9-10 year olds. It therefore comes highly recommended.

**Key Features:**
- Hours of learning and fun at the same time.
- Encourage child's self-confidence in reading.
- Encouraging good handwriting through practice.
- Unique and personalized workbook for your child.
- Easy way to monitor's child's developments and creativity.
- Opportunity for your child's creativity to be developed/enhanced.

**Book details:**
Paperback: 64 pages
Language: English
ISBN: 978-1-908015-03-7

 :www.protokospublishers.co.uk

## ABC of Places and Things in the Bible. (Parent/Teachers Manual 1)

ABC of Places and Things in the Bible (Age 9-10) is the second in a series of Kiddies books specifically designed and written by Oluwakemi Ola-Ojo for children of elementary school age. The book comes as a sequel to ABC of People and Things in the Bible (Age 6-8). It seeks to bridge the gap between parents' desire to educate their children on basic Bible teachings and the ability to pass the information to children of such tender ages in a way they would understand and retain, and in addition, in a manner that will make a positive impact on them.

Like the first in the series, the book offers a highly efficient way of teaching 9-10 year-olds the Bible in a friendly and educative manner. Using the letters of the English alphabet, Oluwakemi Ola-Ojo details key places and things in the Bible, to teach children historical and geographical landmarks of interest as well as objects of significance, not only in ancient biblical times, but also in present day 21st Century.

The book will definitely stir up the imagination of every child

**Key Features:**
Essentially for the present day Parent/Teacher. This manual allows you:
- To learn at the Creator's feet.
- To learn about places and things in the Bible.
- To have wholesome discussions with your child
- To adapt the various teachings to the level of child.
- To teach your child line-upon line, precept –upon - precept
- Gives you many hours of learning and fun together with the child.

**Book details:**
Paperback: 111 pages
Language: English
ISBN: 978-1-908015-02-0

 :www.protokospublishers.co.uk

# INSPIRATIONS FOR THE MAN OF VALOUR

## The Enemy Within
(Destiny Destroyers)

An unusual title! The Enemy Within is yet another mind-boggling piece by Oluwakemi Ola-Ojo. In this book, she draws attention to how our success and/or advancement in life is sometimes impeded or terminated by persons with whom we share close relationships and, by circumstances of life, which are sometimes hereditary or brought upon us by our acts of commission or omission.

Oluwakemi Ola-Ojo takes the discourse from close families such as siblings, parents and spouses to extended relationships such as in-laws, colleagues and bosses in the workplace as well as neighbours and leaders in the nation. The book also explores the effect of such conditions as sickness and poverty as they impact on the human life but concludes that of all of these persons or conditions, the greatest enemy to be conquered is 'self'.

A very interesting and highly educative book that cuts across gender, age and status! It comes highly recommended.

**Book details:**
Paperback: 132 pages
Language: English
ISBN: 978-1-908015-11-2

:www.protokospublishers.co.uk

**COMING OUT SOON**

- INSPIRATIONS FOR THE MAN OF COURAGE.
- MY A.B.C. OF PEOPLE AND THINGS IN THE BIBLE. (SERIES 2)
- MY ABC OF PLACES AND THINGS (SERIES 2)
- TO THE GROOM WITH LOVE.

## USEFUL ADDRESSES & WEBSITES

**Care for the Family**
PO Box 488
Cardiff
CF15 7YY
Tel: (029) 2081 0800
Fax: (029) 2081 4089
Email: mail@cff.org.uk
Website: www.care-for-the-family.org.uk OR www.cff.org.uk
Care for the Family aims to promote strong family life and to help those hurting because of family breakdown. Their heart is to come alongside people in the good times and in the tough times – bringing hope, compassion and some practical, down-to-earth help and encouragement.

**Children Evangelism Ministry Inc**
P.O. Box 4480
Ilorin, Kwara State,
Nigeria.
Tel: +234 31 222199
E-mail: cem@ilorin.skannet.com OR cem562000@yahoo.com
Children Evangelism Ministry Inc is a ministry that reaches out with the Gospel to children before and after birth. The ministry teaches and equips parents, teachers and coordinators of Sunday Schools and Children's Clubs. They also have and hold Children's Clubs, conferences and training seminars.

**Focus on the Family**
Tel: 1-800 - 232 6459
Website: www.family.org
Focus on the Family cooperates with the Holy Spirit in disseminating the Gospel of Jesus Christ to as many people as possible, and, specifically, to accomplish that objective by helping to preserve traditional values and the institution of the family.

**Protokos Publishers**
London, UK
www.protokospublishers.co.uk
(Impacting our community through sharing)
Protokos Publishers provides various resources for the family. We publish many life's enlightening, informative and motivational must read books. With each of our books, you are guaranteed a 24/7 counsellor by your side on the subject.

**The Shepherd's Ministries**
5 Brookehowse Road
Bellingham
London SE6 3TJ, UK
Tel/Fax: +44 208 698 7222
Email: info@theshepherdsministries.org
Website: www.theshepherdsministries.org
The Shepherd's Ministries helps to bring children into an experience of worshipping God in truth and in spirit; give children a world-view based on God's word and mission and helps children to exercise their gifts in local and global missions.

**United Christian Broadcasting UCB**
P.O. Box 255, Stoke on Trent,
ST4 8YY, England
Among other forms of spreading the Gospel, UCB prints The Word For Today – a free daily devotional reading available for residents in the UK and Republic of Ireland

**IN USA:**
www.eCounseling.com
Tel Number: 1-866-268-6735

www.ingramcontent.com/pod-product-compliance
Lightning Source LLC
Chambersburg PA
CBHW071501080526
44587CB00014B/2179